RAMSEY MILHOLLAND

BOOTH TARKINGTON

1st WORLD
LIBRARY
Literary Society

Ramsey Milholland

Booth Tarkington

© 1st World Library, 2007
PO Box 2211
Fairfield, IA 52556
www.1stworldlibrary.com
First Edition

LCCN: 2007934081

Softcover ISBN: 978-1-4218-9618-2
Hardcover ISBN: 978-1-4218-9718-9
eBook ISBN: 978-1-4218-9518-5

Purchase *"Ramsey Milholland"*
as a traditional bound book at:
www.1stWorldLibrary.com/purchase.asp?ISBN=978-1-4218-9618-2

1st World Library is a literary, educational organization dedicated to:

- Creating a free internet library of downloadable ebooks

- Hosting writing competitions and offering book publishing scholarships.

Interested in more 1st World Library books? contact:
literacy@1stworldlibrary.com

Check us out at: www.1stworldlibrary.com

1ˢᵗ World Library Literary Society

Giving Back to the World

"If you want to work on the core problem, it's early school literacy."

- James Barksdale, former CEO of Netscape

"No skill is more crucial to the future of a child, or to a democratic and prosperous society, than literacy."

- Los Angeles Times

"Literacy... means far more than learning how to read and write... The aim is to transmit... knowledge and promote social participation."

- UNESCO

"Literacy is not a luxury, it is a right and a responsibility. If our world is to meet the challenges of the twenty-first century we must harness the energy and creativity of all our citizens."

- President Bill Clinton

"Parents should be encouraged to read to their children, and teachers should be equipped with all available techniques for teaching literacy, so the varying needs and capacities of individual kids can be taken into account."

- Hugh Mackay

To the Memory of Billy Miller (William Henry Harrison Miller II) 1908 - 1918 Little Patriot, Good Citizen Friend of Mankind

CHAPTER I

When Johnnie comes marching home again,
Hurrah! Hurrah!
We'll give him a hearty welcome then,
Hurrah! Hurrah!
The men with the cheers, the boys with shouts,
The ladies they will all turn out,
And we'll all feel gay, when Johnnie comes
marching home again!

The old man and the little boy, his grandson, sat together in the shade of the big walnut tree in the front yard, watching the "Decoration Day Parade," as it passed up the long street; and when the last of the veterans was out of sight the grandfather murmured the words of the tune that came drifting back from the now distant band at the head of the procession.

"Yes, we'll all feel gay when Johnnie comes marching home again," he finished, with a musing chuckle.

"Did you, Grandpa?" the boy asked.

"Did I what?"

"Did you all feel gay when the army got home?"

"It didn't get home all at once, precisely," the grandfather explained. "When the war was over I suppose we felt relieved, more than anything else."

"You didn't feel so gay when the war *was*, though, I guess!" the boy ventured.

"I guess we didn't."

"Were you scared, Grandpa? Were you ever scared the Rebels would win?"

"No. We weren't ever afraid of that."

"Not any at all?"

"No. Not any at all."

"Well, weren't you ever scared yourself, Grandpa? I mean when you were in a battle."

"Oh, yes; *then* I was." The old man laughed. "Scared plenty!"

"I don't see why," the boy said promptly. "I wouldn't be scared in a battle."

"Wouldn't you?"

"'Course not! Grandpa, why don't you march in the Decoration Day Parade? Wouldn't they let you?"

"I'm not able to march any more. Too short of breath and too shaky in the legs and too blind."

Booth Tarkington

"I wouldn't care," said the boy. "I'd be in the parade anyway, if I was you. They had some sittin' in carriages, 'way at the tail end; but I wouldn't like that. If I'd been in your place, Grandpa, and they'd let me be in that parade, I'd been right up by the band. Look, Grandpa! Watch me, Grandpa! This is the way I'd be, Grandpa."

He rose from the garden bench where they sat, and gave a complex imitation of what had most appealed to him as the grandeurs of the procession, his prancing legs simulating those of the horse of the grand marshal, while his upper parts rendered the drums and bugles of the band, as well as the officers and privates of the militia company which had been a feature of the parade. The only thing he left out was the detachment of veterans.

"Putty-boom! Putty-boom! Putty-boom-boom-boom!" he vociferated, as the drums—and then as the bugles: "Ta, ta, ra, tara!" He addressed his restive legs: "*Whoa*, there, you Whitey! Gee! Haw! Git up!" Then, waving an imaginary sword: "Col-lumn right! Farwud *March!* Halt! Carry *harms!*" He "carried arms." "Show-dler *harms!*" He "shouldered arms," and returned to his seat.

"That'd be me, Grandpa. That's the way I'd do." And as the grandfather nodded, seeming to agree, a thought recently dismissed returned to the mind of the composite procession and he asked:

"Well, *why* weren't you ever afraid the Rebels would whip the Unions, Grandpa?"

"Oh, we knew they couldn't."

"I guess so." The little boy laughed disdainfully, thinking his question satisfactorily answered. "I guess those ole Rebels couldn't whipped a flea! They didn't know how to fight any at all, did they, Grandpa?"

"Oh, yes, they did!"

"What?" The boy was astounded. "Weren't they all just reg'lar ole cowards, Grandpa?"

"No," said the grandfather. "They were pretty fine soldiers."

"They were? Well, they ran away whenever you began shootin' at 'em, didn't they?"

"Sometimes they did, but most times they didn't. Sometimes they fought like wildcats—and sometimes we were the ones that ran away."

"What for?"

"To keep from getting killed, or maybe to keep from getting captured."

"But the Rebels were bad men, weren't they, Grandpa?"

"No."

The boy's forehead, customarily vacant, showed some little vertical shadows, produced by a struggle to think. "Well, but—" he began, slowly. "Listen, Grandpa, listen here!"

"Well?"

"Listen! Well, you said—you said you never got scared the ole Rebels were goin' to win."

"They did win pretty often," said the grandfather. "They won

Booth Tarkington

a good many battles."

"I mean, you said you never got scared they'd win the war."

"No, we were never afraid of that."

"Well, but if they were good men and fought like wildcats, Grandpa, and kep' winning battles and everything, how could that be? How could you *help* bein' scared they'd win the war?"

The grandfather's feeble eyes twinkled brightly. "Why, we *knew* they couldn't, Ramsey."

At this, the little vertical shadows on Ramsey's forehead became more pronounced, for he had succeeded in thinking. "Well, *they* didn't know they couldn't, did they?" he argued. "They thought they were goin' to win, didn't they?"

"Yes, I guess they did. Up till toward the last, I suppose they probably did. But you see they were wrong."

"Well, but—" Ramsey struggled. "Listen! Listen here, Grandpa! Well, anyway, if they never got scared *we'd* win, and nobody got scared *they'd* win—well, I don't see—"

"You don't see what?"

But Ramsey found himself unable to continue his concentration; he slumped down upon the small of his back, and his brow relaxed to its more comfortable placidity, while his eyes wandered with a new butterfly fluttering over the irises that bordered the iron picket fence at the south side of the yard. "Oh, nothin' much," he murmured.

"I see." And his grandfather laughed again. "You mean: If

the Rebels felt just as sure of winning the war as we did, and kept winning battles why shouldn't we ever have had any doubts that we were going to win? That's it, isn't it?"

"I guess so, Grandpa."

"Well, I think it was mostly because we were certain that we were right."

"I see," said Ramsey. "The Rebels knew they were on the side of the Devil." But at this, the grandfather's laugh was louder than it had been before, and Ramsey looked hurt. "Well, you can laugh if you want to!" he objected in an aggrieved voice. "Anyway, the Sunday-school sup'intendent told us when people knew they were on the Devil's side they always—"

"I dare say, I dare say," the old man interrupted, a little impatiently. "But in this world mighty few people think they're on the Devil's side, Ramsey. There was a Frenchman once, in olden times; he said people were crazy because, though they couldn't even make worms, they believed they could make gods. And so whenever countries or parts of a country get into a war, each side makes a god and a devil, and says: 'God's on our side and the Devil's on the other.' The South thought the Devil was on our side, you see."

"Well, that kind o' mixes it all up more'n ever."

"Yes, it seems so; but Abraham Lincoln wasn't mixed up about it. When some people told him that God was on our side, he said the important thing was to find out if we were on God's side. That was the whole question, you see; because either side could make up a god, the kind of a god they liked and wanted; and then they'd believe in him, too, and fight for him—but if he was only a made-up god they'd lose.

Booth Tarkington

President Lincoln didn't want to have a made-up god on his side; he wanted to find God Himself and find out what he wanted, and then do it. And that's what Lincoln did."

"Well, I don't understand much of all *that*!"

"No? Then suppose you look at it this way: The South was fighting for what it believed to be its rights, but we weren't fighting for our rights; we were fighting for the right. The South was fighting for what it believed to be its right to split the Union and be a country by itself; but we were fighting for 'Liberty and Union, now and forever, one and inseparable.' It wasn't only the Union we fought for; it was Freedom. The South wanted freedom to leave the Union; but the reason the South wanted that freedom to separate from us was because *we* wanted the Freedom of Man. *There's* the reason we had the certain knowledge that we were going to win the war. How plain and simple it is!"

Ramsey didn't think so. He had begun to feel bored by the conversation, and to undergo the oppression he usually suffered in school; yet he took a little interest in the inexplicable increase of fervour with which his grandfather spoke, and in a shoot of sunshine which somehow got through the foliage of the walnut tree and made a bedazzlement of glinting fine lines in one spot, about the size of a saucer, upon the old man's head of thick white hair. Half closing his eyes, drowsily, Ramsey played that this sunshine spot was a white bird's-next and, and he had a momentary half dream of a glittering little bird that dwelt there and wore a blue soldier cap on its head. The earnest old voice of the veteran was only a sound in the boy's ears.

"Yes, it's simple and plain enough now, though then we didn't often think of it in exactly this way, but just went on fighting and never doubted. We knew the struggle and suffering of our fathers and grandfathers to make a great country here for Freedom, and we knew that all this wasn't just the whim of a foolish god, willing to waste such great things—we knew that such a country couldn't have been building up just to be wasted. But, more than that, we knew that armies fighting for the Freedom of Man *had* to win, in the long run, over armies that fought for what they considered their rights.

"We didn't set out to free the slaves, so far as we knew. Yet our being against slavery was what made the war, and we had the consciousness that we were on the side of God's plan, because His plan is clearly the Freedom of Man. Long ago we began to see the hints of His plan—a little like the way you can see what's coming in August from what happens in April, but man has to win his freedom from himself—men in the light have to fight against men in the dark of their own shadow. That light is the answer; we had the light that made us never doubt. Ours was the true light, and so we—"

"Boom—" The veterans had begun to fire their cannon on the crest of the low hill, out at the cemetery; and from a little way down the street came the rat-a-tat of a toy drum and sounds of a fife played execrably. A file of children in cocked hats made of newspapers came marching importantly up the sidewalk under the maple shade trees; and in advance, upon a velocipede, rode a tin-sworded personage, shrieking incessant commands but not concerning himself with whether or not any military obedience was thereby obtained. Here was a revivifying effect upon young Ramsey; his sluggard eyelids opened electrically; he leaped to his feet and, abandoning his grandfather without preface or apology, sped across the lawn and out of the gate, charging headlong upon the commander of the company.

"You get off that 'locipede, Wesley Bender!" he bellowed. "You gimme that sword! What rights you got to go bein' captain o' my army, I'd like to know! Who got up this army, in the first place, I'd like to know! I did, myself yesterd'y afternoon, and you get back in line or I won't let you b'long to it at all!"

The pretender succumbed; he instantly dismounted, being out-shouted and overawed. On foot he took his place in the ranks, while Ramsey became sternly vociferous. "In-tention, company! Farwud *march*! Col-lumn *right*! Right-showdler *harms*! Halt! Far-wud *march*. Carry harms—"

The Army went trudging away under the continuous but unheed fire of orders, and presently disappeared round a corner, leaving the veteran chuckling feebly under his walnut tree and alone with the empty street. All trace of what he had said seemed to have been wiped from the grandson's mind; but memory has curious ways. Ramsey had understood not a fifth nor a tenth of his grandfather's talk, and already he had "forgotten" all of it—yet not only were there many, many times in the boy's later life when, without ascertainable cause, he would remember the sunlight falling upon the old man's white head, to make that semblance of a glittering bird's-nest there, but with the picture came recollections of words and sentences spoken by the grandfather, though the listener, half-drowsily, had heard but the sound of an old, earnest voice—and even the veteran's meaning finally took on a greater definiteness till it became, in the grandson's thoughts, something clear and bright and beautiful that he knew without being just sure where or how he had learned it.

CHAPTER II

Ramsey Milholland sat miserably in school, his conscious being consisting principally of a dull hate. Torpor was a little dispersed during a fifteen-minute interval of "Music," when he and all the other pupils in the large room of the "Five B. Grade" sang repeated fractions of what they enunciated as "The Star Span-guh-hulled Banner"; but afterward he relapsed into the low spirits and animosity natural to anybody during enforced confinement under instruction. No alleviation was accomplished by an invader's temporary usurpation of the teacher's platform, a brisk and unsympathetically cheerful young woman mounting thereon to "teach German."

For a long time mathematics and German had been about equally repulsive to Ramsey, who found himself daily in the compulsory presence of both; but he was gradually coming to regard German with the greater horror, because, after months of patient mental resistance, he at last began to comprehend that the German language has sixteen special and particular ways of using the German article corresponding to that flexible bit of a word so easily managed English—*the*. What in the world was the use of having sixteen ways of doing a thing that could just as well be done in one? If the Germans had contented themselves with insisting upon sixteen useless variations for infrequent

Booth Tarkington

words, such as *hippopotamus*, for instance, Ramsey might have thought the affair unreasonable but not necessarily vicious—it would be easy enough to avoid talking about a hippopotamus if he ever had to go to Germany. But the fact that the Germans picked out *a* and *the* and many other little words in use all the time, and gave every one of them sixteen forms, and expected Ramsey Milholland to learn this dizzying uselessness down to the last crotchety detail, with "When to employ Which" as a nausea to prepare for the final convulsion when one *didn't* use Which, because it was an "Exception"—there was a fashion of making easy matters hard that was merely hellish.

The teacher was strict but enthusiastic; she told the children, over and over, that German was a beautiful language, and her face always had a glow when she said this. At such times the children looked patient; they supposed it must be so, because she was an adult and their teacher; and they believed her with the same manner of believing which those of them who went to Sunday-school used there when the Sunday-school teachers were pushed into explanations of various matters set forth in the Old Testament, or gave reckless descriptions of heaven. That is to say, the children did not challenge or deny; already they had been driven into habits of resignation and were passing out of the age when childhood is able to reject adult nonsense.

Thus, to Ramsey Milholland, the German language seemed to be a collection of perverse inventions for undeserved torment; it was full of revolting surprises in the way of genders; vocally it often necessitated the employment of noises suggestive of an incompletely mastered knowledge of etiquette; and far inside him there was something faintly but constantly antagonistic to it—yet, when the teacher declared that German was incomparably the most beautiful language in the world, one of the many facets of his mind submissively absorbed the statement as light to be passed inward; it was part of the lesson to be learned. He did not know whether the English language was beautiful or not; he never thought about that, and no one ever said anything to him about it. Moreover, though his deeper inward hated "German," he liked his German teacher, and it was pleasant to look at her when that glow came upon her face.

Sometimes, too, there were moments of relaxation in her class, when she would stop the lesson and tell the children about Germany: what a beautiful, good country it was, so trim and orderly, with such pleasant customs, and all the people sensible and energetic and healthy. There was "Music" again in the German class, which was another alleviation; though it was the same old "Star Spangled Banner" over again. Ramsey was tired of the song and tired of "My Country 'Tis of Thee"; they were bores, but it was amusing to sing them in German. In German they sounded "sort o' funny," so he didn't mind this bit of the day's work.

Half an hour later there arrived his supreme trial of this particular morning. Arithmetic then being the order of business before the house, he was sent alone to the black-board, supposedly to make lucid the proper reply to a fatal conundrum in decimals, and under the glare and focus of the whole room he breathed heavily and itched every-where; his brain at once became sheer hash. He consumed as much time as possible in getting the terms of the problem stated in chalk; then, affecting to be critical of his own handiwork, erased what he had done and carefully wrote it again. After that, he erased half of it, slowly retraced the figures, and stepped back as if to see whether perspective improved their appearance. Again he lifted the eraser.

"Ramsey Milholland!"

"Ma'am?"

"Put down that eraser!"

"Yes'm. I just thought—"

Sharply bidden to get forward with his task, he explained in a feeble voice that he had first to tie a shoe string and stooped to do so, but was not permitted. Miss Ridgely tried to stimulate him with hints and suggestion; found him, so far as decimals went, mere protoplasm, and, wondering how so helpless a thing could live, summoned to the board little Dora Yocum, the star of the class, whereupon Ramsey moved toward his seat.

"Stand still, Ramsey! You stay right where you are and try to learn something from the way Dora does it."

The class giggled, and Ramsey stood, but learned nothing. His conspicuousness was unendurable, because all of his schoolmates naturally found more entertainment in watching him than in following the performance of the capable Dora. He put his hands in and out of his pockets; was bidden to hold them still, also not to shuffle his feet; and when in a false assumption of ease he would have scratched his head Miss Ridgely's severity increased, so that he was compelled to give over the attempt.

Instructed to watch every figure chalked up by the mathematical wonder, his eyes, grown sodden, were unable to remove themselves from the part in her hair at the back of her head, where two little braids began their separate careers to end in a couple of blue-and-red checked bits of ribbon, one upon each of her thin shoulder blades. He was conscious that the part in Dora's shining brown hair was odious, but he was unconscious of anything arithmetical. His sensations clogged his intellect; he suffered from unsought notoriety, and hated Dora Yocum; most of all he hated her busy little shoulder blades.

He had to be "kept in" after school; and when he was allowed to go home he averted his eyes as he went by the house where Dora lived. She was out in the yard, eating a doughnut, and he knew it; but he had passed the age when it is just as permissible to throw a rock at a girl as at a boy; and stifling his normal inclinations, he walked sturdily on, though he indulged himself so far as to engage in a murmured conversation with one of the familiar spirits dwelling somewhere within him. "Pfa!" said Ramsey to himself—or himself to Ramsey, since it is difficult to say which was which. "Pfa! Thinks she's smart, don't she?"... "Well, I guess she does, but she ain't!" ... "I hate her, don't you?"... "You bet your life I hate her!"... "Teacher's Pet, that's what *I* call her!"... "Well, that's what *I* call her, too, don't I?" "Well, *I* do; that's all she is, anyway—dirty ole Teacher's Pet!"

CHAPTER III

He had not forgiven her four years later when he entered high school in her company, for somehow Ramsey managed to shovel his way through examinations and stayed with the class. By this time he had a long accumulation of reasons for hating her: Dora's persistent and increasing competency was not short of flamboyant, and teachers naturally got the habit of flinging their quickest pupil in the face of their slowest and "dumbest." Nevertheless, Ramsey was unable to deny that she had become less awful lookin' than she used to be. At least, he was honest enough to make a partial retraction when his friend and classmate, Fred Mitchell, insisted that an amelioration of Dora's appearance could be actually proven.

"Well, I'll take it back. I don't claim she's every last bit as awful lookin' as she always has been," said Ramsey, toward the conclusion of the argument. "I'll say this for her, she's awful lookin', but she may not be as awful lookin' as she was. She don't come to school with the edge of some of her underclo'es showin' below her dress any more, about every other day, and her eyewinkers have got to stickin' out some, and she may not be so abbasa*loot*ly skinny, but she'll haf to wait a mighty long while before *I* want to look at her without gettin' sick!"

The implication that Miss Yocum cared to have Ramsey look

at her, either with or without gettin' sick, was mere rhetoric, and recognized as such by the producer of it; she had never given the slightest evidence of any desire that his gaze be bent upon her. What truth lay underneath his flourish rested upon the fact that he could not look at her without some symptoms of the sort he had tersely sketched to his friend; and yet, so pungent is the fascination of self-inflicted misery, he did look at her, during periods of study, often for three or four minutes at a stretch. His expression at such times indeed resembled that of one who has dined unwisely; but Dora Yocum was always too eagerly busy to notice it. He was almost never in her eye, but she was continually in his; moreover, as the banner pupil she was with hourly frequency an exhibit before the whole class.

Ramsey found her worst of all when her turn came in "Declamation," on Friday afternoons. When she ascended the platform, bobbed a little preliminary bow and began, "Listen, my children, and you shall hear," Ramsey included Paul Revere and the Old North Church and the whole Revolutionary War in his antipathy, since they somehow appeared to be the property of the Teacher's Pet. For Dora held this post in "Declamation" as well as in everything else; here, as elsewhere, the hateful child's prowess surpassed that of all others; and the teacher always entrusted her with the rendition of the "patriotic selections": Dora seemed to take fire herself when she declared:

"The fate of a nation was riding that night;
And the spark struck out by that steed in his flight,
Kindled the land into flame with its heat."

Ramsey himself was in the same section of declaimers, and performed next—a ghastly contrast. He gave a "selection from Shakespeare," assigned by the teacher; and he began this continuous misfortune by stumbling violently as he ascended the platform, which stimulated a general giggle already in being at the mere calling of his name. All of the class were bright with happy anticipation, for the miserable Ramsey seldom failed their hopes, particularly in "Declamation." He faced them, his complexion wan, his expression both baleful and horrified; and he began in a loud, hurried voice, from which every hint of intelligence was excluded:

"Most pottent, grave, and rev—"

The teacher tapped sharply on her desk, and stopped him. "You've forgotten to bow," she said. "And don't say 'pottent.' The word is 'potent'."

Ramsey flopped his head at the rear wall of the room, and began again:

"Most pottent potent gray and revenerd signers my very nobe and approve good masters that I have tan away this sole man's dutter it is mose true true I have marry dur the very headman frun tuv my fending hath this extent no more rude am I in speech—in speech—rude am I in speech—in speech—in speech—in speech—"

He had stalled. Perhaps the fatal truth of that phrase, and some sense of its applicability to the occasion had interfered with the mechanism which he had set in operation to get rid of the "recitation" for him. At all events, the machine had to run off its job all at once, or it wouldn't run at all. Stopped, it stayed stopped, and backing off granted no new impetus, though he tried, again and again. "Hath this extent no more rude am I in speech—" He gulped audibly. "Rude rude rude am I—rude am I in speech—in speech—in speech. Rude am I in speech—"

"Yes," the irritated teacher said, as Ramsey's failing voice continued huskily to insist upon this point. "I think you are!" And her nerves were a little soothed by the shout of laughter from the school—it was never difficult for teachers to be witty. "Go sit down, Ramsey, and do it after school."

His ears roaring, the unfortunate went to his seat, and, among all the hilarious faces, one stood out—Dora Yocum's. Her laughter was precocious; it was that of a confirmed superior, insufferably adult—she was laughing at him as a grown person laughs at a child. Conspicuously and unmistakably, there was something indulgent in her amusement. He choked. Here was a little squirt of a high-school girl who would trot up to George Washington himself and show off around him, given the opportunity; and George Washington would probably pat her on the head, or give her a medal—or something. Well, let him! Ramsey didn't care. He didn't care for George Washington, or Paul Revere, or Shakespeare, or any of 'em. They could all go to the dickens with Dora Yocum. They were all a lot of smarties anyway and he hated the whole stew of 'em!

There was one, however, whom he somehow couldn't manage to hate, even though this one officially seemed to be as intimately associated with Dora Yocum and superiority as the others were. Ramsey couldn't hate Abraham Lincoln, even when Dora was chosen to deliver the "Gettysburg Address" on the twelfth of February. Vaguely, yet reassuringly, Ramsey felt that Lincoln had resisted adoption by the intellectuals. Lincoln had said "Government of the people, by the people, for the people," and that didn't mean government by the teacher and the Teacher's Pet and Paul Revere and Shakespeare and suchlike; it meant government by everybody, and therefore Ramsey had as much to do with it as anybody else had. This was friendly; and he believed that if Abraham Lincoln could have walked into the schoolroom, Lincoln would have been as friendly with him as with Dora and the teacher herself. Beyond a doubt, Dora and the teacher *thought* Lincoln belonged to them and their crowd of exclusives; they seemed to think they owned the whole United States; but Ramsey was sure they were mistaken about Abraham Lincoln.

He felt that it was just like this little Yocum snippet to assume such a thing, and it made him sicker than ever to look at her.

Then, one day, he noticed that her eye-winkers were stickin' out farther and farther.

CHAPTER IV

His discovery irritated him the more. Next thing, this ole Teacher's Pet would do she'd get to thinkin' she was pretty! If *that* happened, well, nobody *could* stand her! The long lashes made her eyes shadowy, and it was a fact that her shoulder blades ceased to insist upon notoriety; you couldn't tell where they were at all, any more. Her back seemed to be just a regular back, not made up of a lot of implements like shoulder blades and things.

A contemptible thing happened. Wesley Bender was well known to be the most untidy boy in the class and had never shown any remorse for his reputation or made the slightest effort either to improve or to dispute it. He was content: it failed to lower his standing with his fellows or to impress them unfavourably. In fact, he was treated as one who has attained a slight distinction. At least, he owned one superlative, no matter what its quality, and it lifted him out of the commonplace. It helped him to become better known, and boys liked to be seen with him. But one day, there was a rearrangement of the seating in the schoolroom: Wesley Bender was given a desk next in front of Dora Yocum's; and within a week the whole room knew that Wesley had begun voluntarily to wash his neck—the back of it, anyhow.

This was at the bottom of the fight between Ramsey

Milholland and Wesley Bender, and the diplomatic exchanges immediately preceding hostilities were charmingly frank and unhyprocitical, although quite as mixed-up and off-the-issue as if they had been prepared by professional foreign office men. Ramsey and Fred Mitchell and four other boys waylaid young Bender on the street after school, intending jocosities rather than violence, but the victim proved sensitive. "You take your ole hands off o' me!" he said fiercely, as they began to push him about among them.

"Ole dirty Wes!" they hoarsely bellowed and squawked, in their changing voices. "Washes his ears!"... "Washes his *neck!*"... "Dora Yocum told his mama to turn the hose on him!"... "Yay-ho! Ole dirty Wes tryin to be a duke!"

Wesley broke from them and backed away, swinging his strapped books in a dangerous circle. "You keep off!" he warned them. "I got as much right to my pers'nal appearance as anybody!"

This richly fed their humour, and they rioted round him, keeping outside the swinging books at the end of the strap. "Pers'nal appearance!"... "Who went and bought it for you, Wes?"... "Nobody bought it for him. Dora Yocum took and give him one!"

"You leave ladies' names alone!" cried the chivalrous Wesley. "You ought to know better, on the public street, you—pups!"

Here was a serious affront, at least to Ramsey Milholland's way of thinking; for Ramsey, also, now proved sensitive. He quoted his friends—"Shut up!"—and advanced toward Wesley. "You look here! Who you callin' 'pups'?"

"Everybody!" Wesley hotly returned. "Everybody that hasn't

got any more decency than to go around mentioning ladies' names on the public streets. Everybody that goes around mentioning ladies' names on the public streets are pups!"

"They are, are they?" Ramsey as hotly demanded. "Well, you just look here a minute; my own father mentions my mother's name on the public streets whenever he wants to, and you just try callin' my father a pup, and you won't know what happened to you!"

"What'll *you* do about it?"

"I'll put a new head on you," said Ramsey. "That's what I'll do, because anybody that calls my father or mother a pup—"

"Oh, shut up! I wasn't talking about your ole father and mother. I said everybody that mentioned Dora Yocum's name on the public streets was a pup, and I mean it! Everybody that mentions Dora Yocum's name on the pub—"

"Dora Yocum!" said Ramsey. "I got a perfect right to say it anywhere I want to. Dora Yocum, Dora Yocum, Dora Yocum!—"

"All right, then you're a pup!"

Ramsey charged upon him and received a suffocating blow full in the face, not from Mr. Bender's fist but from the solid bundle of books at the end of the strap. Ramsey saw eight or ten objectives instantly: there were Wesley Benders standing full length in the air on top of other Wesley Benders, and more Wesley Benders zigzagged out sideways from still other Wesley Benders; nevertheless, he found one of these and it proved to be flesh. He engaged it wildly at fisticuffs; pounded it upon the countenance and drove it away. Then he sat down upon the curbstone, and, with his dizzy eyes shut, leaned forward for the better accommodation of his ensanguined nose.

Wesley had retreated to the other side of the street holding a grimy handkerchief to the midmost parts of his pallid face. "There, you ole damn pup!" he shouted, in a voice which threatened to sob. "I guess *that'll* teach you to be careful how you mention Dora Yocum's name on the public streets!"

At this, Ramsey made a motion as if to rise and pursue, whereupon Wesley fled, wailing back over his shoulder as he ran, "You wait till I ketch you out alone on the public streets and I'll—"

His voice was lost in an outburst of hooting from his former friends, who sympathetically surrounded the wounded Ramsey. But in a measure, at least, the chivalrous fugitive had won his point. He was routed and outdone, yet what survived the day was a rumour, which became a sort of tenuous legend among those interested. There had been a fight over Dora Yocum, it appeared, and Ramsey Milholland had attempted to maintain something derogatory to the lady, while Wesley defended her as a knightly youth should. The something derogatory was left vague; nobody attempted to say just what it was, and the effects of the legend divided the schoolroom strictly according to gender.

The boys, unmindful of proper gallantry, supported Ramsey on account of the way he had persisted in lickin' the stuffin' out of Wesley Bender after receiving that preliminary wallop from Wesley's blackjack bundle of books. The girls petted and championed Wesley; they talked outrageously of his conqueror, fiercely declaring that he ought to be arrested; and for weeks they maintained a new manner toward him. They kept their facial expressions hostile, but perhaps this was more for one another's benefit than for Ramsey's; and several of them went so far out of their way to find even private opportunities for reproving him that an alert observer might have suspected them to have been less indignant than they seemed—but not Ramsey. He thought they all hated him, and said he was glad of it.

Dora was a non-partisan. The little prig was so diligent at her books she gave never the slightest sign of comprehending that there had been a fight about her. Having no real cognizance of Messrs. Bender and Milholland except as impediments to the advance of learning, she did not even look demure.

CHAPTER V

With Wesley Bender, Ramsey was again upon fair terms before the winter had run its course; the two were neighbours and, moreover, were drawn together by a community of interests which made their reconciliation a necessity. Ramsey played the guitar and Wesley played the mandolin.

All ill feeling between them died with the first duet of spring, yet the twinkling they made had no charm to soothe the savage breast of Ramsey whenever the Teacher's Pet came into his thoughts. He daydreamed a thousand ways of putting her in her place, but was unable to carry out any of them, and had but a cobwebby satisfaction in imagining discomfitures for her which remained imaginary. With a yearning so poignant that it hurt, he yearned and yearned to show her what she really was. "Just once!" he said to Fred Mitchell. "That's all I ask, just once. Just gimme one chance to show that girl what she really is. I guess if I ever get the chance she'll find out what's the matter with her, for *once* in her life, anyway!" Thus it came to be talked about and understood and expected in Ramsey's circle, all male, that Dora Yocum's day was coming. The nature of the disaster was left vague, but there was no doubt in the world that retribution merely awaited its ideal opportunity. "You'll see!" said Ramsey. "The time'll come when that ole girl'll wish she'd moved o' this town before she ever got appointed monitor of *our* class! Just you wait!"

They waited, but conditions appeared to remain unfavourable indefinitely. Perhaps the great opportunity might have arrived if Ramsey had been able to achieve a startling importance in any of the "various divergent yet parallel lines of school endeavour"—one of the phrases by means of which teachers and principal clogged the minds of their unarmed auditors. But though he was far from being the dumb driven beast of misfortune that he seemed in the schoolroom, and, in fact, lived a double life, exhibiting in his out-of-school hours a remarkable example of "secondary personality"—a creature fearing nothing and capable of laughter; blue-eyed, fairly robust, and anything but dumb—he was nevertheless without endowment or attainment great enough to get him distinction.

He "tried for" the high-school eleven, and "tried for" the nine, but the experts were not long in eliminating him from either of these competitions, and he had to content himself with cheering instead of getting cheered. He was by no manner of means athlete enough, or enough of anything else, to put Dora Yocum in her place, and so he and the great opportunity were still waiting in May, at the end of the second year of high school, when the class, now the "10 A," reverted to an old fashion and decided to entertain itself with a woodland picnic.

They gathered upon the sandy banks of a creek, in the blue shade of big, patchy-barked sycamores, with a dancing sky on top of everything and gold dust atwinkle over the water. Hither the napkin-covered baskets were brought from the wagons and assembled in the shade, where they appeared as an attractive little meadow of white napery, and gave both surprise and pleasure to communities of ants and to other original settlers of the neighbourhood.

From this nucleus or headquarters of the picnic, various expeditions set forth up and down the creek and through the woods that bordered it. Camera work was constant; spring wild flowers were accumulated by groups of girls who trooped through the woods with eager eyes searching the thickets; two envied boy fishermen established themselves upon a bank up-stream, with hooks and lines thoughtfully brought with them, and poles which they fashioned from young saplings. They took mussels from the shallows, for bait, and having gone to all this trouble, declined to share with friends less energetic and provident the perquisites and pleasures secured to themselves.

Albert Paxton was another person who proved his enterprise. Having visited the spot some days before, he had hired for his exclusive use throughout the duration of the picnic an old rowboat belonging to a shanty squatter; it was the only rowboat within a mile or two and Albert had his own uses for it. Albert was the class lover and, after first taking the three chaperon teachers "out for a row," an excursion concluded in about ten minutes, he disembarked them; Sadie Clews stepped into the boat, a pocket camera in one hand, a tennis racket in the other; and the two spent the rest of the day, except for the luncheon interval, solemnly drifting along the banks or grounded on a shoal. Now and then Albert would row a few strokes, and at almost any time when the populated shore glanced toward them, Sadie would be seen photographing Albert, or Albert would be seen photographing Sadie, but the tennis racket remained an enigma. Oarsman and passenger appeared to have no conversation whatever—not once was either seen or heard to address a remark to the other; and they looked as placid as their own upside-down reflections in one of the still pools they slowly floated over. They were sixteen, and had been "engaged" more than two years.

On the borders of the little meadow of baskets there had been deposited two black shapes, which remained undisturbed throughout the day, a closed guitar case and a closed mandolin case, no doubt containing each its proper instrument. So far as any use of these went they seemed to be of the same leisure class to which Sadie's tennis racket belonged, for when one of the teachers suggested music, the musicians proved shy. Wesley Bender said they hadn't learned to play anything much and, besides, he had a couple o' broken strings he didn't know as he could fix up; and Ramsey said he guessed it seemed kind o' too hot to play much. Joining friends, they organized a contest in marksmanship, the target being a floating can which they assailed with pebbles; and after that they "skipped" flat stones upon the surface of the water, then went to join a group gathered about Willis Parker and Heinie Krusemeyer.

No fish had been caught, a lack of luck crossly attributed by the fishermen to the noise made by constant advice on the part of their attendant gallery. Messrs. Milholland, Bender, and the other rock throwers came up shouting, and were ill received.

"For heaven's sakes," Heinie Krusemeyer demanded, "can't you shut up? Here we just first got the girls to keep their mouths shut a minute and I almost had a big pickerel or something on my hook, and here you got to up and yell so he chases himself away! Why can't nobody show a little sense sometimes when they ought to?"

"I should say so!" his comrade exclaimed. "If people would only just take and think of all the trouble we been to, it seems funny somebody couldn't let us have half a chance to get a few good fish. What chance they got to bite with a lot o' *girls* gabbin' away, and then, just as we get 'em quieted down, all you men got to come bustin' up here yellin' your heads off. A fish isn't goin' to bite when he can't even hear himself think! Anybody ought to know that much."

But the new arrivals hooted. *"Fish!"* Ramsey vociferated. "I'll bet a hundred dollars there hasn't been even a minny in this creek for the last sixty years!"

"There is, too!" said Heinie, bitterly. "But I wouldn't be surprised there wouldn't be no longer if you got to keep up this noise. If you'd shut up just a minute you could see yourself there's fish here."

In whispers several of the tamed girls at once heartily corroborated this statement, whereupon the newcomers ceased to gibe and consented to silence. Ramsey leaned forth over the edge of the overhanging bank, a dirt precipice five feet above the water, and peered into the indeterminable depths below. The pool had been stirred, partly by the inexpert pokings of the fishermen and partly by small clods and bits of dirt dislodged from above by the feet of the audience. The water, consequently, was but brownly translucent and revealed its secrets reluctantly; nevertheless certain dim little shapes had been observed to move within it, and were still there. Ramsey failed to see them at first.

"Where's any ole fish?" he inquired, scornfully.

"Oh, my goodness!" Heinie Krusemeyer moaned. "*Can't* you shut up?"

"Look!" whispered the girl who stood nearest to Ramsey. She pointed. "There's one. Right down there by Willis's hook. Don't you see him?"

Ramsey was impressed enough to whisper. "Is there? I don't see him. I can't—"

The girl came closer to him, and, the better to show him, leaned out over the edge of the bank, and, for safety in maintaining her balance, rested her left hand upon his shoulder while she pointed with her right. Thereupon something happened to Ramsey. The touch upon his shoulder was almost nothing, and he had never taken the slightest interest in Milla Rust (to whom that small warm hand belonged), though she was the class beauty, and long established in the office. Now, all at once, a peculiar and heretofore entirely unfamiliar sensation suddenly became important in the upper part of his chest. For a moment he held his breath, an involuntary action;—he seemed to be standing in a shower of flowers.

"Don't you see it, Ramsey?" Milla whispered. "It's a great big one. Why, it must be as long as—as your shoe! Look!"

Ramsey saw nothing but the thick round curl on Milla's shoulder. Milla had a group of curls on each of her shoulders, for she got her modes at the Movies and had that sort of prettiness: large, gentle, calculating eyes, and a full, softly modelled face, implacably sweet. Ramsey was accustomed to all this charm, and Milla had never before been of more importance to him than an equal weight of school furniture—but all at once some magic had enveloped her. That curl upon the shoulder nearest him was shot with dazzling fibres of sunshine. He seemed to be trembling.

"I don't see it," he murmured, huskily, afraid that she might remove her hand. "I can't see any fish, Milla."

She leaned farther out over the bank. "Why, there, goosie!" she whispered. "Right there."

"I can't see it."

She leaned still farther, bending down to point. "Why right th—"

At this moment she removed her hand from his shoulder, though unwillingly. She clutched at him, in fact, but without avail. She had been too amiable.

A loud shriek was uttered by throats abler to vocalize, just then, than Milla's, for in her great surprise she said nothing whatever—the shriek came from the other girls as Milla left the crest of the overhanging bank and almost horizontally disappeared into the brown water. There was a tumultuous splash, and then of Milla Rust and her well-known beautifulness there was nothing visible in the superficial world, nor upon the surface of that creek. The vanishment was total.

"*Save* her!"

Several girls afterward admitted having used this expression, and little Miss Floy Williams, the youngest and smallest member of the class, was unable to deny that she had said, "Oh, God!" Nothing could have been more natural, and the matter need not have been brought before her with such insistence and frequency, during the two remaining years of her undergraduate career.

Ramsey was one of those who heard this exclamation, later so famous, and perhaps it was what roused him to heroism. He dived from the bank, headlong, and the strange thought in his mind was "I guess *this*'ll show Dora Yocum!" He should have been thinking of Milla, of course, at such a time, particularly after the little enchantment just laid upon him by Milla's touch and Milla's curls; and he knew well enough that Miss Yocum was not among the spectators. She was half a mile away, as it happened, gathering "botanical specimens" with one of the teachers—which was her idea of what to do at a picnic!

Ramsey struck the water hard, and in the same instant struck something harder. Wesley Bender's bundle of books had given him no such shock as he received now, and if the creek bottom had not been of mud, just there, the top of his young head might have declined the strain. Half stunned, choking, spluttering he somehow floundered to his feet; and when he could get his eyes a little cleared of water he found himself wavering face to face with a blurred vision of Milla Rust. She had risen up out of the pod and stood knee deep, like a lovely drenched figure in a fountain.

Upon the bank above them, Willis Parker was jumping up and down, gesticulating and shouting fiercely. "Now I guess you're satisfied our fishin' *is* spoilt! Whyn't you listen me? I *told* you it wasn't more'n three feet deep! I and Heinie waded all over this creek gettin' our bait. You're a pretty sight!"

Of Milla he spoke unwittingly the literal truth. Even with her hair thus wild and sodden, Milla rose from immersion blushing and prettier than ever; and she was prettiest of all when she stretched out her hand helplessly to Ramsey and he led her up out of the waters. They had plenty of assistance to scramble to the top of the bank, and there Milla was surrounded and borne away with a great clacketing and tumult. Ramsey gave his coat into the hands of friends, who twisted the water out of it for him, while he sat upon the grass in the sun, rubbed his head, and experimented with his neck to see if it would "work." The sunshine was strong and hot; in half an hour he and his clothes were dry—or at least "dry enough," as he said, and except for some soreness of head and neck, and the general crumpledness of his apparel, he seemed to be in all ways much as usual when shouts and whistlings summoned all the party to luncheon at the rendezvous. The change that made him different was invisible.

CHAPTER VI

The change in Ramsey was invisible, and yet something must have been seen, for everyone appeared to take it for granted that he was to sit next to Milla at the pastoral meal. She herself understood it, evidently, for she drew in her puckered skirts and without any words make a place for him beside her as he driftingly approached her, affecting to whistle and keeping his eyes on the foliage overhead. He still looked upward, even in the act of sitting down.

"Squirrel or something," he said, feebly, as if in explanation.

"Where?" Milla asked.

"Up there on a branch." He accepted a plate from her (she had provided herself with an extra one), but he did not look at it or her. "I'm not just exactly sure it's a squirrel," he said. "Kind of hard to make out exactly what it is." He continued to keep his eyes aloft, because he imagined that all of the class were looking at him and Milla, and he felt unable to meet such publicity. It was to him as if the whole United States had been scandalized to attention by this act of his in going to sit beside Milla; he gazed upward so long that his eyeballs became sensitive under the strain. He began to blink. "I can't make out whether it's a squirrel or just some leaves that kind o' got fixed like one," he said. "I can't make out yet which it is, but I guess when there's a breeze, if it's a squirrel he'll prob'ly hop around some then, if he's alive or anything."

It had begun to seem that his eyes must remain fixed in that upward stare forever; he wanted to bring them down, but could not face the glare of the world. So the fugitive ostrich is said to bury his head in the sand; he does it, not believing himself thereby hidden but trying to banish from his own cognizance terrible facts which his unsheltered eyes have seemed to reveal. So, too, do nervous children seek to bury their eyes under pillows, and nervous statesmen theirs under oratory. Ramsey's ostrichings can happen to anybody. But finally the brightness of the sky between the leaves settled matters for him; he sneezed, wept, and for a little moment again faced his fellowmen. No one was looking at him; everybody except Milla had other things to do.

Having sneezed involuntarily, he added a spell of coughing for which there was no necessity. "I guess I must be wrong," he muttered thickly.

"What about, Ramsey?"

"About it bein' a squirrel." With infinite timidity he turned his head and encountered a gaze so soft, so hallowed, that it disconcerted him, and he dropped a "drumstick" of fried chicken, well dotted with ants, from his plate. Scarlet he picked it up, but did not eat it. For the first time in his life he felt that eating fried chicken held in the fingers was not to be thought of. He replaced the "drumstick" upon his plate and allowed it to remain there untouched, in spite of a great hunger for it.

Having looked down, he now found difficulty in looking up, but gazed steadily at his plate, and into this limited circle of vision came Milla's delicate and rosy fingers, bearing a gift. "There," she said in a motherly little voice. "It's a tomato mayonnaise sandwich and I made it myself. I want you to eat it, Ramsey."

His own fingers approached tremulousness as he accepted the thick sandwich from her and conveyed it to his mouth. A moment later his soul filled with horror, for a spurt of mayonnaise dressing had caused a catastrophe the scene of which occupied no inconsiderable area of his right cheek; which was the cheek toward Milla. He groped wretchedly for his handkerchief but could not find it; he had lost it. Sudden death would have been relief; he was sure that after such grotesquerie Milla could never bear to have anything more to do with him; he was ruined.

In his anguish he felt a paper napkin pressed gently into his hand; a soft voice said in his ear, "Wipe it off with this, Ramsey. Nobody's noticing."

So this incredibly charitable creature was still able to be his friend, even after seeing him mayonnaised! Humbly marvelling, he did as she told him, but avoided all further risks. He ate nothing more.

He sighed his first sigh of inexpressibleness, had a chill or so along the spine, and at intervals his brow was bedewed.

Within his averted eyes there dwelt not the Milla Rust who sat beside him, but an iridescent, fragile creature who had become angelic.

He spent the rest of the day dawdling helplessly about her; wherever she went he was near, as near as possible, but of no deliberate volition of his own. Something seemed to tie him to her, and Milla was nothing loth. He seldom looked at her directly, or for longer than an instant, and more rarely still did he speak to her except as a reply. What few remarks he ventured upon his own initiative nearly all concerned the landscape, which he commended repeatedly in a weak voice, as "kind of pretty," though once he said he guessed there might be bugs in the bark of a log on which they sat; and he became so immoderately personal as to declare that if the bugs had to get on anybody he'd rather they got on him than on Milla. She said that was "just perfectly lovely" of him, asked where he got his sweet nature, and in other ways encouraged him to continue the revelation, but Ramsey was unable to get forward with it, though he opened and closed his mouth a great many times in the effort to do so.

At five o'clock everybody was summoned again to the rendezvous for a ceremony preliminary to departure: the class found itself in a large circle, standing, and sang "The Star Spangled Banner." Ordinarily, on such an open-air and out-of-school occasion, Ramsey would have joined the chorus uproariously with the utmost blatancy of which his vocal apparatus was capable; and most of the other boys expressed their humour by drowning out the serious efforts of the girls; but he sang feebly, not much more than humming through his teeth. Standing beside Milla, he was incapable of his former inelegancies and his voice was in a semi-paralyzed condition, like the rest of him.

Opposite him, across the circle, Dora Yocum stood a little in advance of those near her, for of course she led the singing. Her clear and earnest voice was distinguishable from all others, and though she did not glance toward Ramsey he had a queer feeling that she was assuming more superiority than ever, and that she was icily scornful of him and Milla. The old resentment rose—he'd "show" that girl yet, some day!

When the song was over, cheers were given for the class,

"the good ole class of Nineteen Fourteen," the school, the teachers, and for the picnic, thus officially concluded; and then the picnickers, carrying their baskets and faded wild flowers and other souvenirs and burdens, moved toward the big "express wagons" which were to take them back into the town. Ramsey got his guitar case, and turned to Milla.

"Well—" he said.

"Well what, Ramsey?"

"Well—g'bye."

"Why, no," said Milla. "Anyways not yet. You can go back in the same wagon with me. It's going to stop at the school and let us out there, and then you could walk home with me if you felt like it. You could come all the way to our gate with me, I expect, unless you'd be late home for your supper."

"Well—well, I'd be perfectly willing," Ramsey said. "Only I heard we all had to go back in whatever wagon we came out in, and I didn't come in the same wagon with you, so—"

Milla laughed and leaned toward him a little. "I already 'tended to that," she said confidentially. "I asked Johnnie Fiske, that came out in my wagon, to go back in yours, so that makes room for you."

"Well—then I guess I could do it." He moved toward the wagon with her. "I expect it don't make much difference one way or the other."

"And you can carry my basket if you want to," she said, adding solicitously, "Unless it's too heavy when you already got your guitar case to carry, Ramsey."

This thoughtfulness of hers almost overcame him; she seemed divine. He gulped, and emotion made him even pinker than he had been under the mayonnaise.

"I—I'll be glad to carry the basket, too," he faltered. "It-it don't weigh anything much."

"Well, let's hurry, so's we can get places together."

Then, as she manoeuvred him through the little crowd about the wagon, with a soft push this way and a gentle pull that, and hurried him up the improvised steps and found a place where there was room for them to sit, Ramsey had another breathless sensation heretofore unknown to him. He found himself taken under a dovelike protectorship; a wonderful, inexpressible Being seemed to have become his proprietor.

"Isn't this just perfectly lovely?" she said cozily, close to his ear.

He swallowed, but found no words, for he had no thoughts; he was only an incoherent tumult. This was his first love.

"Isn't it, Ramsey?" she urged. The cozy voice had just the hint of a reproach. "Don't you think it's just perfectly lovely, Ramsey?"

"Yes'm."

CHAPTER VII

The next morning Ramsey came into his father's room while Mr. Milholland was shaving, an hour before church time, and it became apparent that the son had someting on his mind, though for a while he said nothing.

"Did you want anything, Ramsey?"

"Well—"

"Didn't want to borrow my razors?"

"No, sir."

Mr. Milholland chuckled. "I hardly supposed so, seriously! Shaving is a great nuisance and the longer you keep away from it, the better. And when you do, you let my razors alone, young feller!"

"Yes, sir." (Mr. Milholland's razors were safe, Ramsey had already achieved one of his own, but he practised the art in secret.) He passed his hand thoughtfully over his cheeks, and traces of white powder were left upon his fingers, whereupon he wiped his hand surreptitiously, and stood irresolutely waiting.

"What is it you really want, Ramsey?"

"I guess I don't want anything."

"Money?"

"No, sir. You gay' me some Friday."

Mr. Milholland turned from his mirror and looked over the edge of a towel at his son. In the boy's eyes there was such a dumb agony of interrogation that the father was a little startled.

"Why, what is it, Ramsey? Have you—" He paused, frowning and wondering. "You haven't been getting into some mess you want to tell me about, have you?"

"No, sir."

His tone was meek, but a mute distress lurked within it, bringing to the father's mind disturbing suspicions, and foreshadowings of indignation and of pity. "See here, Ramsey," he said, "if there's anything you want to ask me, or to tell me, you'd better out with it and get it over. Now, what is it?"

"Well—it isn't anything."

"Are you *sure?*"

Ramsey's eyes fell before the severe and piercing gaze of his father. "Yes, sir."

Mr. Milholland shook his head doubtfully; then, as his son walked slowly out of the room, he turned to complete his toilet in a somewhat uneasy frame of mind. Ramsey had undoubtedly wanted to say something to him and the boy's expression had shown that the matter in question was serious, distressing, and, it might be, even critical.

In fact it was—to Ramsey. Having begun within only the last few hours to regard haberdashery as of vital importance, and believing his father to be possessed of the experience and authority lacking in himself, Ramsey had come to get him to settle a question which had been upsetting him badly, in his own room, since breakfast. What he want to know was: Whether it was right to wear an extra handkerchief showing out of the coat breast pocket or not, and, if it was right— ought the handkerchief to have a coloured border or to be plain white? But he had never before brought any such perplexities to his father, and found himself too diffident to set them forth.

However, when he left the house, a few minutes later, he boldly showed an inch of purple border above the pocket; then, as he was himself about to encounter several old lady pedestrians, he blushed and thrust the handkerchief down into deep concealment. Having gone a block farther, he pulled it up again; and so continued to operate this badge of fashion, or unfashion, throughout the morning; and suffered a great deal thereby.

Meantime, his father, rather relieved that Ramsey had not told his secret, whatever it was, dismissed the episode from his mind and joined Mrs. Milholland at the front door, ready for church.

"Where's Ramsey?" he asked.

"He's gone ahead," she answered, buttoning her gloves as they went along. "I heard the door quite a little while ago. Perhaps he went over to walk down with Charlotte and Vance. Did you notice how neat he looks this morning?"

"Why, no, I didn't; not particularly. Does he?"

"I never saw anything like it before," said Mrs. Milholland. "He went down in the cellar and polished his own shoes."

"What!"

"For about an hour, I think," she said, as one remaining calm before a miracle. "And he only has three neckties, but I saw him several times in each of them. He must have kept changing and changing. I wonder—" She paused.

"I'm glad he's begun to take a little care of his appearance at last. Business men think a good deal about that, these days, when he comes to make his start in the world. I'll have to take a look at him and give him a word of praise. I suppose he'll be in the pew when we get there."

But Ramsey wasn't in the pew; and Charlotte, his sister, and her husband, who were there, said they hadn't seen anything of him. It was not until the members of the family were on their way home after the services that they caught a glimpse of him.

They were passing a church a little distance from their own; here the congregation was just emerging to the open, and among the sedate throng descending the broad stone steps appeared an accompanied Ramsey—and a red, red Ramsey he was when he beheld his father and mother and sister and brother-in-law staring up at him from the pavement below. They were kind enough not to come to an absolute halt, but passed slowly on, so that he was just able to avoid parading up the street in front of them. The expressions of his father, mother, and sister were of a dumfoundedness painful to bear, while such lurking jocosity as that apparent all over his brother-in-law no dignified man should either exhibit or be called upon to ignore.

In hoarse whispers, Mrs. Milholland chided her husband for an exclamation he had uttered. "John! On Sunday! You ought to be ashamed."

"I couldn't help it," he exclaimed. "Who on earth is his clinging vine? Why, she's got *lavender* tops on her shoes and—"

"Don't look round!" she warned him sharply. "Don't—"

"Well, what's he doing at a Baptist church? What's he fidgeting at his handkerchief about? Why can't he walk like people? Does he think it's obligatory to walk home from church anchored arm-in-arm like Swedes on a Sunday Out? Who *is* this cow-eyed fat girl that's got him, anyhow?"

"Hush! Don't look round again, John."

"Never fear!" said her husband, having disobeyed. "They've turned off; they're crossing over to Bullard Street. Who is it?"

"I think her name's Rust," Mrs. Milholland informed him. "I don't know what her father does. She's one of the girls in his class at school."

"Well, that's just like a boy; pick out some putty-faced flirt to take to church!"

"Oh, she's quite pretty—in that way!" said his wife, deprecatingly. "Of course that's the danger with public schools. It would be pleasanter if he'd taken a fancy to someone whose family belongs to our own circle."

"'Taken a fancy'!" he echoed, hooting. "Why, he's terrible! He looked like a red-gilled goldfish that's flopped itself out of the bowl. Why, he—"

"I *say* I wish if he felt that he had to take girls anywhere," said Mrs. Milholland, with the primmest air of speaking to the point—"if this sort of thing *must* begin, I wish he might have selected some nice girl among the daughters of our own friends, like Dora Yocum, for instance."

Upon the spot she began to undergo the mortification of a mother who has expected her son, just out of infancy, to look about him with the eye of a critical matron of forty-five. Moreover, she was indiscreet enough to express her views to Ramsey, a week later, producing thus a scene of useless great fury and no little sound.

"I do think it's in *very* poor taste to see so much of any one girl, Ramsey," she said, and, not heeding his protest that he only walked home from school with Milla, "about every other day," and that it didn't seem any crime to him just to go to church with her a couple o' times, Mrs. Milholland went on: "But if you think you really *must* be dangling around somebody quite this much—though what in the world you find to *talk* about with this funny little Milla Rust you poor father says he really cannot see—and of course it seems very queer to us that you'd be willing to waste so much time just now when your mind ought to be entirely on your studies, and especially with such an absurd *looking* little thing—

"No, you must listen, Ramsey, and let me speak now. What I meant was that we shouldn't be *quite* so much distressed by your being seen with a girl who dressed in better taste and seemed to have some notion of refinement, though of course it's only natural she *wouldn't*, with a father who is just a sort of ward politician, I understand, and a mother we don't know, and of course shouldn't care to. But, oh, Ramsey! if you *had* to make yourself so conspicuous why couldn't you be a little *bit* more fastidious? Your father wouldn't have minded nearly so much if it had been a self-respecting, intellectual girl. We both say that if you *must* be so ridiculous at your age as to persist in seeing more of one girl than another, why, oh why, don't you go and see some really nice girl like Dora Yocum?"

Ramsey was already dangerously distended, as an effect of the earlier part of her discourse, and the word "fastidious" almost exploded him; but upon the climax, "Dora Yocum," he blew up with a shattering report and, leaving fragments of incoherence ricocheting behind him, fled shuddering from the house.

For the rest of the school term he walked home with Milla every afternoon and on sundays appeared to have become a resolute Baptist. It was supposed (by the interested members of the high-school class) that Ramsey and Milla were "engaged." Ramsey sometimes rather supposed they were himself, and the dim idea gave him a sensation partly pleasant, but mostly apprehensive: he was afraid.

He was afraid that the day was coming when he ought to kiss her.

CHAPTER VIII

Vacation, in spite of increased leisure, may bring inconvenience to people in Ramsey's strange but not uncommon condition. At home his constant air was that of a badgered captive plaintively silent under injustice; and he found it difficult to reply calmly when asked where he was going—an inquiry addressed to him, he asserted, every time he touched his cap, even to hang it up!

The amount of evening walking he did must also have been a trial to his nerves, on account of fatigue, though the ground covered was not vast. Milla's mother and father were friendly people but saw no reason to "move out of house and home," as Mr. Rust said, when Milla had "callers"; and on account of the intimate plan of their small dwelling a visitor's only alternative to spending the evening with Mr. and Mrs. Rust as well as with Milla, was to invite her to "go out walking."

Evening after evening they walked and walked and walked, usually in company—at perhaps the distance of half a block—with Albert Paxton and Sadie Clews, though Ramsey now and then felt disgraced by having fallen into this class; for sometimes it was apparent that Albert casually had his arm about Sadie's waist. This allured Ramsey somewhat, but terrified him more. He didn't know how such matters were managed.

Usually the quartet had no destination; they just went "out walking" until ten o'clock, when both girls had to be home— and the boys did, too, but never admitted it. On Friday evenings there was a "public open-air concert" by a brass band in a small park, and the four were always there. A political speechmaker occupied the bandstand one night, and they stood for an hour in the midst of the crowd, listening vaguely.

The orator saddled his politics upon patriotism. "Do you intend to let this glorious country go to wrack and ruin, oh, my good friends," he demanded, "or do you intend to save her? Look forth upon this country of ours, I bid you, oh, my countrymen, and tell me what you see. You see a fair domain of forest, mountain, plain, and fertile valleys, sweeping from ocean to ocean. Look from the sturdy rocks of old New England, pledged to posterity by the stern religious hardi-hood of the Pilgrim Fathers, across the corn-bearing midland country, that land of milk and honey, won for us by the pluck and endurance of the indomitable pioneers, to where in sunshine roll the smiling Sierras of golden California, given to our heritage by the unconquerable energy of those brave men and women who braved the tomahawk on the Great Plains, the tempest, of Cape Horn, and the fevers of Panama, to make American soil of El Dorado! America! Oh, my America, how glorious you stand! Country of Washington and Valley Forge, out of what martyrdoms hast thou arisen! Country of Lincoln in his box at Ford's theatre, his lifeblood staining to a brighter, holier red the red, white, and blue of the Old Flag! Always and always I see the Old Flag fluttering the more sacredly encrimsoned in the breeze for the martyrs who have upheld it! Always I see that Old Flag—"

Milla gave Ramsey's arm, within her own, a little tug. "Come on," she said. "Sade says she don't want to hang around here any longer. It's awful tiresome. Let's go."

He consented, placidly. The oration meant nothing to him and stirred no one in the audience. The orator was impassioned; he shouted himself into coughing fits, gesticulated, grew purple; he was so hot that his collar caved in and finally swooned upon his neck in soggy exhaustion, prostrate round his thunderings. Meanwhile, the people listened with an air of patience, yawning here and there, and gradually growing fewer. It was the old, old usual thing, made up of phrases that Ramsey had heard dinning away on a thousand such occasions, and other kinds of occasions, until they meant to him no more than so much sound. He was bored, and glad to leave.

"Kind o' funny," he said, as they sagged along the street at their usual tortoise gait.

"What is it, Ramsey?"

"Seems kind o' funny they never have anything to say any one can take any interest in. Always the same ole whoopety-whoop about George Washington and Pilgrim Fathers and so on. I bet five dollars before long we'd of heard him goin' on about our martyred Presidents, William McKinley and James A. Garfield and Benjamin Harrison and all so on, and then some more about the ole Red, White, and Blue. Don't you wish they'd *quit*, sometimes, about the 'Ole Flag'?"

"I dunno," said Milla. "I wasn't listening any at all. I hate speeches."

"Well, I could *stand* 'em," Ramsey said, more generously, "if they'd ever give anybody a little to think about. What's the use always draggin' in George Warshington and the Ole Flag? And who wants to hear any more ole truck about 'from ole rocky New England to golden California,' and how big and fine the United States is and how it's the land of the Free and all that? Why don't they ever say anything new? That's what I'd like to know."

Milla laughed, and when he asked why, she told him she'd never heard him talk so much "at one stretch." "I guess that speech got you kind of wound up," she said. "Let's talk about something different."

"I just soon," he agreed. And so they walked on in silence, which seemed to suit Milla. She hung weightily upon his arm, and they dawdled, drifting from one side of the pavement to the other as they slowly advanced. Ablert and Sadie, ahead of them, called "good-night" from a corner, before turning down the side street where Sadie lived; and then, presently, Ramsey and Milla were at the latter's gate. He went in with her, halting at the front steps.

"Well, g'night, Milla," he said. "Want to go out walking to-morrow night? Albert and Sadie are."

"I can't to-morrow night," she told him with obvious regret. "Isn't it the worst luck! I got an aunt comin' to visit from Chicago, and she's crazy about playing 'Five Hundred,' and Mama and Papa said I haf to stay in to make four to play it. She's liable to be here three or four days, and I guess I got to be around home pretty much all the time she's here. It's the worst luck!"

He was doleful, but ventured to be literary. "Well, what can't be helped must be endured. I'll come around when she's gone."

He moved as if to depart, but she still retained his arm and did not prepare to relinquish it.

"Well—" he said.

"Well what, Ramsey?"

"Well—g'night."

She glanced up at the dark front of the house. "I guess the family's gone to bed," she said, absently.

"I s'pose so."

"Well, good-night, Ramsey." She said this but still did not release his arm, and suddenly, in a fluster, he felt that the time he dreaded had come. Somehow, without knowing where, except that it was somewhere upon what seemed to be a blurred face too full of obstructing features, he kissed her.

She turned instantly away in the darkness, her hands over her cheeks; and in a panic Ramsey wondered if he hadn't made a dreadful mistake.

"S'cuse me!" he said, stumbling toward the gate. "Well, I guess I got to be gettin' along back home."

CHAPTER IX

He woke in the morning to a great self-loathing: he had kissed a girl. Mingled with the loathing was a curious pride in the very fact that caused the loathing, but the pride did not last long. He came downstairs morbid to breakfast, and continued this mood afterward. At noon Albert Paxton brought him a note which Milla had asked Sadie to ask Albert to give him.

Dearie: I am just wondering if you thought as much about something so sweet that happened last night as I did you know what. I think it was the sweetest thing. I send you one with this note and I hope you will think it is a sweet one. I would give you a real one if you were here now and I hope you would think it was sweeter still than the one I put in this note. It is the sweetest thing now you are mine and I am yours forever kiddo. If you come around about friday eve it will be all right. aunt Jess will be gone back home by then so come early and we will get Sade and Alb and go to the band Concert. Don't forget what I said about my putting something sweet in this note, and I hope you will think it is a sweet one but not as sweet as the *real* sweet one I would like to—

At this point Ramsey impulsively tore the note into small pieces. He turned cold as his imagination projected a sketch of his mother in the act of reading this missive, and of her expression as she read the sentence: "It is the sweetest thing now you are mine and I am yours forever kiddo." He wished that Milla hadn't written "kiddo." She called him that, sometimes, but in her warm little voice the word seemed not at all what it did in ink. He wished, too, that she hadn't said she was his forever.

Suddenly he was seized with a horror of her.

Moisture broke out heavily upon him; he felt a definite sickness, and, wishing for death, went forth upon the streets to walk and walk. He cared not whither, so that his feet took him in any direction away from Milla, since they were unable to take him away from himself—of whom he had as great a horror. Her loving face was continually before him, and its sweetness made his flesh creep. Milla had been too sweet.

When he met or passed people, it seemed to him that perhaps they were able to recognize upon him somewhere the marks of his low quality. "Softy! Ole sloppy fool!" he muttered, addressing himself. "Slushy ole mush!... *Spooner!*" And he added, "Yours forever, kiddo!" Convulsions seemed about to seize him.

Turning a corner with his head down, he almost charged into Dora Yocum. She was homeward bound from a piano lesson, and carried a rolled leather case of sheet music—something he couldn't imagine Milla carrying—and in her young girl's dress, which attempted to be nothing else, she looked as wholesome as cold spring water. Ramsey had always felt that she despised him and now, all at once, he thought that she was justified. Leper that he had become, he was unworthy to be even touching his cap to her! And as she nodded and went briskly on, he would have given anything to turn and walk a little way with her, for it seemed to him that this might fumigate his morals. But he lacked the courage, and, besides, he considered himself unfit to be seen walking with her.

He had a long afternoon of anguishes, these becoming most violent when he tried to face the problem of his future course toward Milla. He did not face it at all, in fact, but merely writhed, and had evolved nothing when Friday evening was upon him and Milla waiting for him to take her to the "band concert" with "Alb and Sade." In his thoughts, by that time, this harmless young pair shared the contamination of his own crime, and he regarded them with aversion; however, he made shift to seek a short interview with Albert, just before dinner.

"I got a pretty rotten headache, and my stomach's upset, too," he said, drooping upon the Paxton's fence. "I been gettin' worse every minute. You and Sadie go by Milla's, Albert, and tell her if I'm not there by ha'-pas'-seven, tell her not to wait for me any longer."

"How do you mean 'wait'?" Albert inquired. "You don't expect her to come pokin' along with Sadie and me, do you? She'll keep on sittin' there at home just the same, because she wouldn't have anything else to do, if you don't come like she expects you to. She hasn't got any way to *stop* waitin'!"

At this, Ramsey moaned, without affectation. "I don't expect I *can*, Albert," he said. "I'd like to if I could, but the way it looks now, you tell her I wouldn't be much surprised maybe I was startin' in with typhoid fever or pretty near anything at all. You tell her I'm pretty near as disappointed as she's goin' to be herself, and I'd come if I could—and I *will* come if I get a good deal better, or anything—but the way it's gettin' to look now, I kind o' feel as if I might be breaking out with something any minute." He moved away, concluding, feebly: "I guess I better crawl on home, Albert, while I'm still able to walk some. You tell her the way it looks now I'm liable to be right sick."

And the next morning he woke to the chafings of remorse, picturing a Milla somewhat restored in charm waiting hopefully at the gate, even after half-past seven, and then, as time passed and the sound of the distant horns came faintly through the darkness, going sadly to her room—perhaps weeping there. It was a picture to wring him with shame and pity, but was followed by another which electrified him, for out of school he did not lack imagination. What if Albert had reported his illness too vividly to Milla? Milla was so fond! What if, in her alarm, she should come here to the house to inquire of his mother about him? What if she told Mrs. Milholland they were "engaged"? The next moment Ramsey was projecting a conversation between his mother and Milla in which the latter stated that she and Ramsey were soon to be married; that she regarded him as already virtually her husband, and demanded to nurse him.

In a panic he fled from the house before breakfast, going out by way of a side door, and he crossed back yards and climbed back fences to reach Albert Paxton the more swiftly. This creature, a ladies' man almost professionally, was found exercising with an electric iron and a pair of flannel trousers in a basement laundry, by way of stirring his appetite for the morning meal.

"See here, Albert," his friend said breathlessly. "I got a favour. I want you to go over to Milla's—"

"I'm goin' to finish pressin' these trousers," Albert interrupted. "Then I've got my breakfast to eat."

"Well, you could do this first," said Ramsey, hurriedly. "It wouldn't hurt you to do me this little favour first. You just slip over and see Milla for me, if she's up yet, and if she isn't, you better wait around there till she is, because I want you to tell her I'm a whole lot better this morning. Tell her I'm pretty near practick'ly all right again, Albert, and I'll prob'ly write her a note or something right soon—or in a week or so, anyhow. You tell her—"

"Well, you act pretty funny!" Albert exclaimed, fumbling in the pockets of his coat. "Why can't you go on over and tell her yourself?"

"I would," said Ramsey. "I'd be perfectly willing to go only I got to get back home to breakfast."

Albert stared. "Well, I got to go upstairs and eat my own breakfast in about a minute, haven't I? But just as it happens there wouldn't be any use your goin' over there, or me, either."

"Why not?"

"Milla ain't there," said Albert, still searching the pockets of his coat. "When we went by her house last night to tell her about your headache and stomach and all, why, her mother told us Milla'd gone up to Chicago yesterday afternoon with her aunt, and said she left a note for you, and she said if you were sick I better take it and give it to you. I was goin' to bring it over to your house after breakfast." He found it. "Here!"

Ramsey thanked him feebly, and departed in a state of partial stupefaction, brought on by a glimpse of the instabilities of life. He had also, not relief, but a sense of vacancy and loss; for Milla, out of his reach, once more became mysteriously lovely.

Pausing in an alley, he read her note.

Dearie: Thought I ought to call you up but over the 'phone is just nix for explanations as Mama and Aunt Jess would hear everything and thought I might seem cold to you not saying anything sweet on account of them listening and you would wonder why I was so cold when telling you good-by for a wile maybe weeks. It is this way Uncle Purv wired Aunt Jess he has just taken in a big touring car on a debt and his vacation starts to-morrow so if they were going to take a trip they better start right way so Aunt Jess invited me. It is going to be a big trip up around the lakes and I have always wanted to go touring more than anything in the world stopping at hotels and all and Mama said I ought to it would be so splendid for my health as she thinks I am failing some lately. Now dearie I have to pack and write this in a hurry so you will not be disappointed when you come by for the B. C. to-night. Do not go get some other girl and take her for I would hate her and nothing in this world make me false for one second to my kiddo boy. I do not know just when home again as the folks think I better stay up there for a visit at Aunt Jess and Uncle Purvs home in Chicago after the trip is over. But I will think of you all the time and you must think of me every minute and believe your own dearie she will never no not for one second be false. So tell Sade and Alb good-by for me and do not be false to me any more than I would be to you and it will not be long till nothing more will interrupt our sweet friendship.

As a measure of domestic prudence, Ramsey tore the note into irreparable fragments, but he did this slowly, and without experiencing any of the revulsion created by Milla's former missive.

He was melancholy, aggrieved that she should treat him so.

Booth Tarkington

CHAPTER X

He never saw her again. She sent him a "picture postal" from Oconomowoc, Wisconsin, which his father disengaged from the family mail, one morning at breakfast, and considerately handed to him without audible comment. Upon it was written, *"Oh, you Ramsey!"* This was the last of Milla.

Just before school opened, in the autumn, Sadie Clews made some revelations. "Milla did like you," said Sadie. "After that time you jumped in the creek to save her she liked you better than any boy in town, and I guess if it wasn't for her cousin Milt up in Chicago she would of liked you the best anywhere. I guess she did, anyway, because she hadn't seen him for about a year then.

"Well, that afternoon she went away I was over there and took in everything that was goin' on, only she made me promise on my word of honour I wouldn't even tell Albert. They didn't get any wire from her uncle about the touring car; it was her cousin Milt that jumped on the train and came down and fixed it all up for Milla to go on the trip, and everything. You see, Ramsey, she was turned back a couple of times in school before she came in our class and I don't exactly know how old she is and she don't *look* old yet, but I'm pretty sure she's at least eighteen, and she might be over. Her mother kept tellin' her all the time you were just a kid, and didn't have anything to support her on, and lots of things like that. I didn't think such a great deal of this Milt's looks, myself, but he's anyway twenty-one years old, and got a good position, and all their family seem to think he's just fine! It wasn't his father that took in the touring car on debt, like she said she was writing to you; it was Milt himself. He started out in business when he was only fifteen years old, and this trip he was gettin' up for his father and mother and Milla was the first vacation he ever took. Well, of course she wouldn't like my tellin' you, but I can't see the harm of it, now everything's all over."

"All—all over? You mean Milla's going to be—to be married?"

"She already is," said Sadie. "They got married at her Aunt Jess and Uncle Purv's house, up in Chicago, last Thursday. Yes, sir; that quiet little Milla's a regular old married woman by this time, I expect, Ramsey!"

When he got over the shock, which was not until the next day, one predominating feeling remained: it was a gloomy pride—a pride in his proven maturity. He was old enough, it appeared, to have been the same thing as engaged to a person who was now a Married Woman. His manner thenceforth showed an added trace of seriousness and self-consideration.

Having recovered his equipoise and something more, he entirely forgot that moment of humble admiration he had felt for Dora Yocum on the day of his flattest prostration. When he saw her sitting in the classroom, smiling brightly up at the teacher, the morning of the school's opening in the autumn, all his humility had long since vanished and she appeared to him not otherwise than as the scholar whose complete proficiency had always been so irksome to him.

"Look at her!" he muttered to himself. "Same ole Teacher's Pet!"

Now and then, as the days and seasons passed, and Dora's serene progress continued, never checked or even flawed, there stirred within some lingerings of the old determination to "show" her; and he would conjure up a day-dream of Dora in loud lamentation, while he led the laughter of the spectators. But gradually his feelings about her came to be merely a dull oppression. He was tired of having to look at her (as he stated it) and he thanked the Lord that the time wouldn't be so long now until he'd be out of that ole school, and then all he'd have to do he'd just take care never to walk by her house; it was easy enough to use some other street when he had to go down-town.

"The good ole class of Nineteen-Fourteen is about gone," he said to Fred Mitchell, who was still his most intimate friend when they reached the senior year. "Yes, sir; it's held together a good many years, Fred, but after June it'll be busted plum up, and I hope nobody starts a move to have any reunions. There's a good many members of the ole class that I can stand and there's some I can't, but there's one I just won't! If we ever did call a reunion, that ole Yocum girl would start in right away and run the whole shebang, and that's where I'd resign! You know, Fred, the thing *I* think is the one biggest benefit of graduating from this ole school? It's never seein' Dora Yocum again."

This was again his theme as he sat by the same friend's side, in the rear row of the class at Commencement, listening to the delivery of the Valedictory. "Thinks she's just sooblime, don't she!" he whispered morosely. "She wouldn't trade with the President of the United States right now. She prob'ly thinks bein' Valedictorian is more important than Captain of the State University Eleven. Never mind!" And here his tone became huskily jubilant. "Never mind! Just about a half-an-hour more and that's the last o' *you*, ole girl! Yes, sir, Fred; one thing we can feel pretty good over: this is where we get through with Dora Yocum!"

Ramsey and Fred had arranged to room together at Greenfield, the seat of the state university, and they made the short journey in company the following September. They arrived hilarious, anticipating pleasurable excitements in the way of "fraternity" pledgings and initiations, encounters with sophomores, class meetings, and elections; and, also, they were not absolutely without interest in the matter of Girls, for the state university was co-educational, and it was but natural to expect in so broad a field, all new to them, a possible vision of something rather thrilling. They whispered cheerfully of all these things during the process of matriculation, and signed the registrar's book on a fresh page; but when Fred had written his name under Ramsey's, and blotted it, he took the liberty of turning over the leaf to examine some of the autographs of their future classmates, written on the other side. Then he uttered an exclamation, more droll than dolorous, though it affected to be wholly the latter; for the shock to Fred was by no means so painful as it was to his friend.

Ramsey leaned forward and read the name indicated by Fred's forefinger.

Dora Yocum.

...When they got back to their pleasant quarters at Mrs. Meig's, facing the campus, Ramsey was still unable to talk of anything except the lamentable discovery; nor were his companion's burlesquing efforts to console him of great avail, though Fred did become serious enough to point out that a university was different from a high school.

"It's not like havin' to use one big room as a headquarters, you know, Ramsey. Everything's all split up, and she might happen not to be in a single of your classes."

"You don't know my luck!" the afflicted boy protested. "I wish I'd gone to Harvard, the way my father wanted me to. Why, this is just the worst nuisance I ever struck! You'll see! She'll be in everything there is, just the way she was back home."

He appeared to be corroborated by the events of the next day, when they attended the first meeting to organize the new class. The masculine element predominated, but Dora Yocum was elected vice-president. "You see?" Ramsey said. "Didn't I tell you? You see what happens?"

But after that she ceased for a time to intrude upon his life, and he admitted that his harassment was less grave than he had anticipated. There were about five hundred students in the freshman class; he seldom saw her, and when he did it was not more than a distant glimpse of her on one of the campus paths, her thoughtful head bent over a book as she hurried to a classroom. This was bearable; and in the flattering agitations of being sought, and even hunted, by several "fraternities" simultaneously desirous of his becoming a sworn Brother, he almost forgot her. After a hazardous month the roommates fell into the arms of the last "frat" to seek them, and having undergone an evening of outrage which concluded with touching rhetoric and an oath taken at midnight, they proudly wore jewelled symbols on their breasts and were free to turn part of their attention to other affairs, especially the affairs of the Eleven.

However, they were instructed by the older brethren of their Order, whose duty it was to assist in the proper manoeuvring of their young careers, that, although support of the 'varsity teams was important, they must neglect neither the spiritual nor the intellectual by-products of undergraduate doings. Therefore they became members of the college Y.M.C.A. and of the "Lumen Society."

According to the charter which it had granted itself, the "Lumen Society" was an "Organization of male and female students"—so "advanced" was this university—"for the development of the powers of debate and oratory, intellectual and sociological progress, and the discussion of all matters relating to philosophy, metaphysics, literature, art, and current events." A statement so formidable was not without a hushing effect upon Messrs. Milholland and Mitchell; they went to their first "Lumen" meeting in a state of fear and came away little reassured.

"I couldn't get up there," Ramsey declared, "I couldn't stand up there before all that crowd and make a speech, or debate in a debate, to save my soul and gizzard! Why, I'd just keel right over and haf to be carried out."

"Well, the way I understand it," said Fred, "we can't get out of it. The seniors in the 'frat' said we had to join, and they said we couldn't resign, either, after we had joined. They said we just had to go through it, and after a while we'd get used to it and not mind it much."

"*I* will!" Ramsey insisted. "I couldn't any more stand up there on my feet and get to spoutin' about sociology and the radical metempsychorus of the metaphysical bazoozum than I could fly a flyin' machine. Why, I—"

"Oh, that wasn't anything," Fred interrupted. "The only one that talked like that, he was that Blickens; he's a tutor, or something, and really a member of the faculty. Most o' the others just kind of blah-blahhed around, and what any of 'em tried to get off their chests hardly amounted to terribly much."

"I don't care. I couldn't do it at *all!*"

"Well, the way it looks to me," Fred observed, "we simply *got* to! From what they tell me, the freshmen got to do more than anybody. Every other Friday night, it's all freshmen and nothin' else. You get a postal card on Monday morning in your mail, and it says 'Assignment' on it, and then it's got written underneath what you haf to do the next Friday night —oration or debate, or maybe just read from some old book or something. I guess we got to stand up there and *try*, anyway."

"All right," said Ramsey. "If they want me to commit suicide they can send me one o' their ole 'Assignments.' I won't need to commit suicide, though, I guess. All I'll do, I'll just fall over in a fit, and stay in it."

And, in truth, when he received his first "Assignment," one Monday morning, a month later, he seemed in a fair way to fulfil his prophecy. The attention of his roommate, who sat at a window of their study, was attracted by sounds of strangulation.

"What on earth's the matter, Ramsey?"

"Look! Look at *this!*"

Fred took the card and examined it with an amazement gradually merging into a pleasure altogether too perceptible:

ASSIGNMENT

TWELVE-MINUTE DEBATE, CLASS OF 1918. *Subject,*

Resolved: That Germany is both legally and morally justified in her invasion of Belgium.

(Debaters are notified that each will be held strictly to the following schedule: Affirmative, 4 min., first. Negative, 4 min., first. Affirm, 2 min., second. Neg., 2 min., second.)

Affirmative Negative R. MILHOLLAND, '18 D. YOCUM, '18

Concluding his reading, which was oral, the volatile Mitchell made use of his voice in a manner of heathenish boisterousness, and presently reclined upon a lounge to laugh the better. His stricken comrade, meanwhile, recovered so far as to pace the floor. "I'm goin' to pack up and light out for home!" he declared, over and over. And even oftener he read and reread the card to make sure of the actuality of that fatal coincidence, "D. Yocum, '18."

CHAPTER XI

"If I *could* do it," he vociferated, "if I *could* stand up there and debate one o' their darn ole debates in the first place—if I had the gall to even try it, why, my gosh! you don't suppose I'm goin' to get up there and argue with *that girl*, do you? That's a hot way to get an education: stand up there and argue with a girl before a couple o' hundred people! My *gosh!*"

"You got to!" his prostrate companion cackled, weakly. "You can't get out of it. You're a goner, ole Buddy!"

"I'll be sick. I'll be sick as a dog! I'll be sick as the sickest dog that ever—"

"No use, ole man. The frat seniors'll be on the job. They'll know whether you're sick or not, and they'll have you there, right on the spot to the minute!"

The prediction was accurate. The too fatherly "frat seniors" did all that Fred said they would, and more. For the honour of the "frat," they coached the desperate Ramsey in the technic of Lumen debate, told him many more things to say than could be said in six minutes, and produced him, despairing, ghastly, and bedewed, in the large hall of the Lumen Society at eight o'clock on Friday evening.

Four other "twelve-minute debates" preceded his and the sound of these, in Ramsey's ears, was the sound of Gabriel practising on his horn in the early morning of Judgment Day. The members of the society sat, three rows deep, along the walls of the room, leaving a clear oblong of green carpet in the centre, where were two small desks, twenty feet apart, the rostrums of the debaters. Upon a platform at the head of the room sat dreadful seniors, the officers of the society, and, upon benches near the platform, the debaters of the evening were aligned. One of the fraternal seniors sat with sweltering Ramsey; and the latter, as his time relentlessly came nearer, made a last miserable squirm.

"Look here, Brother Colburn, I got to get out o' here."

"No, you don't, young fellow."

"Yes, I do!" Ramsey whispered, passionately. "Honest, I do. Honest, Brother Colburn, I got to get a drink of water. I *got* to!"

"No. You can't."

"Honest, Colburn, I *got*—"

"Hush!"

Ramsey grunted feebly, and cast his dilating eyes along the rows of faces. Most of them were but as blurs, swimming, yet he was aware (he thought) of a formidable and horrible impassive scrutiny of himself, a glare seeming to pierce through him to the back of the belt round his waist, so that he began to have fearful doubts about that belt, about every fastening and adjustment of his garments, about the expression of his countenance, and about many other things jumbling together in his consciousness. Over and over he whispered gaspingly to himself the opening words of the sentence with which Colburn had advised him to begin his argument. And as the moment of supreme agony drew close, this whispering became continuous: "In making my first appearance before this honor'ble membership I feel constrained to say in making my first appearance before this honor'ble membership I feel constrained to say in making my first appearance before this honor'ble mem—"

...It had come. The chairman announced the subject of the fourth freshman twelve-minute debate; and Dora Yocum, hitherto unperceived by Ramsey, rose and went forward to one of the small desks in the open space, where she stood composedly, a slim, pretty figure in white. Members in Ramsey's neighbourhood were aware of a brief and hushed commotion, and of Colburn's fierce whisper, "You can't! You get up there!" And the blanched Ramsey came forth and placed himself at the other desk.

He stood before the silent populace of that morgue, and it seemed to him that his features had forgotten that he was supposed to be their owner and in control of them; he felt that they were slipping all over his face, regardless of his wishes. His head, as a whole, was subject to an agitation not before known by him; it desired to move rustily in eccentric ways of its own devising; his legs alternately limbered and straightened under no direction but their own; and his hands clutched each other fiercely behind his back; he was not one cohesive person, evidently, but an assembled collection of parts which had relapsed each into its own individuality. In spite of them, he somehow contrived the semblance of a bow toward the chairman and the semblance of another toward Dora, of whom he was but hazily conscious. Then he opened his mouth, and, not knowing how he had started his voice going, heard it as if from a distance.

"In making my first appearance before this honor'ble membership I feel restrained to say—" He stopped short, and thenceforward shook visibly. After a long pause, he managed to repeat his opening, stopped again, swallowed many times, produced a handkerchief and wiped his face, an act of necessity—then had an inspiration.

"The subject assigned to me," he said, "is resolved that Germany is mor'ly and legally justified in Belgians— Belgiums! This subject was assigned to me to be the subject of this debate." He interrupted himself to gasp piteously; found breathing difficult, but faltered again: "This subject is the subject. It is the subject that was assigned to me on a postal card." Then, for a moment or so, he had a miraculous spurt of confidence, and continued rather rapidly: "I feel constrained to say that the country of Belgian—Belgium, I mean—this country has been constrained by the—invaded I mean—invaded by the imperial German Impire and my subject in this debate is whether it ought to or not, my being the infernative—affirmative, I mean—that I got to prove that Germany is mor'ly and legally justified. I wish to state that—"

He paused again, lengthily, then struggled on. "I have been requested to state that the German Imp—Empire—that it certainly isn't right for those Dutch—Germans, I mean—they haven't got any more business in Belgium than I have myself, but I—I feel constrained to say that I had to accept whatever side of this debate I got on the postal card, and so I am constrained to take the side of the Dutch. I mean the Germans. The Dutch are sometimes called—I mean the Germans are sometimes called the Dutch in this country, but they aren't Dutch, though sometimes called Dutch in this country. Well, and so—so, well, the war began last August or about then, anyway, and the German army invaded the Belgian army. After they got there, the invasion began. First, they came around there and then they commenced invading.

Well, what I feel constrained—"

He came to the longest of all his pauses here, and the awful gravity of the audience almost suffocated him. "Well," he concluded, "it don't look right to me."

"Four minutes!" the chairman announced, for Ramsey's pauses had worn away a great deal more of this terrible interval than had his eloquence. "Opening statement for the negative: Miss D. Yocum. Four minutes."

As Dora began to speak, Ramsey experienced a little relief, but only a little—about the same amount of relief as that felt by a bridegroom when it is the bride's turn to "respond," not really relief at all, but merely the slight relaxation of a continuing strain. The audience now looked at Ramsey no more than people look at a bridegroom, but he failed to perceive any substantial mitigation of his frightful conspicuousness. He had not the remotest idea of what he had said in setting forth his case for Germany, and he knew that it was his duty to listen closely to Dora, in order to be able to refute her argument when his two-minute closing speech fell due but he was conscious of little more than his own condition. His legs had now gone wild beyond all devilry, and he had to keep shifting his weight from one to the other in order even to hope that their frenzy might escape general attention.

He realized that Dora was speaking rapidly and confidently, and that somewhere in his ill-assembled parts lurked a familiar bit of him that objected to her even more than usual; but she had used half of her time, at least, before he was able to gather any coherent meaning from what she was saying. Even then he caught only a fragment, here and there, and for the rest—so far as Ramsey was concerned—she might as well have been reciting the Swedish alphabet.

In spite of the rather startling feebleness of her opponent's statement, Dora went at her task as earnestly as if it were to confute some monster of casuistry. "Thus, having demonstrated that *all* war is wrong," she said, approaching her conclusion, "it is scarcely necessary to point out that whatever the actual circumstances of the invasion, and whatever the status of the case in international law, or by reason of treaty, or the German oath to respect the neutrality of Belgium, which of course was grossly and dishonorably violated—all this, I say, ladies and gentlemen of the Lumen Society, all this is beside the point of morals. Since, as I have shown, *all* war is wrong, the case may be simplified as follows: All war is morally wrong. *Quod erat demonstrandum*. Germany invaded Belgium. Invasion is war. Germany, therefore, did moral wrong. Upon the legal side, as I began by pointing out, Germany confessed in the Reichstag the violation of law. Therefore, Germany was justified in the invasion neither morally nor legally; but was both morally and legally wrong and evil. Ladies and gentlemen of the Lumen Society, I await the refutation of my opponent!"

Her opponent appeared to be having enough trouble with his legs, without taking any added cares upon himself in the way of refutations. But the marvellous Dora had calculated the length of her statement with such nicety that the chairman announced "Four minutes," almost upon the instant of her final syllable; and all faces turned once more to the upholder of the affirmative. "Refutation and conclusion by the affirmative," said the chairman. "Mr. R. Milholland. Two minutes."

Therewith, Ramsey coughed as long as he could cough, and when he felt that no more should be done in this way, he wiped his face—again an act of necessity—and quaveringly began:

"Gentlemen and ladies, or ladies and gentlemen, in making the refutation of my opponent, I feel that—I feel that hardly anything more ought to be said."

He paused, looked helplessly at his uncontrollable legs, and resumed: "I am supposed to make the reputa—the refutation of my opponent, and I feel that I ought to say quite a good deal more. In the first place, I feel that the invasion has taken place. I am supposed—anyhow I got a postal card that I am supposed to be here to-night. Well, in talking over this matter with a couple of seniors, they told me I was supposed to claim this invasion was mor'ly and legally all right. Well—" Here, by some chance, the recollection of a word of Dora's flickered into his chaotic mind, and he had a brighter moment. "My opponent said she proved all war is wrong—or something like that, anyhow. She said she proved it was wrong to fight, no matter what. Well, if she wasn't a girl, anybody that wanted to get her into a fight could prob'ly do it." He did not add that he would like to be the person to make the experiment (if Dora weren't a girl), nor did the thought enter his mind until an hour or so later. "Well," he added, "I suppose there is little more to be said."

He was so right, in regard to his own performance, at least, that, thereupon drying up utterly, he proceeded to stand, a speechless figure in the midst of a multitudinous silence, for an eternity lasting forty-five seconds. He made a racking effort, and at the end of this epoch found words again. "In making my argument in this debate, I would state that—"

"Two minutes!" said the chairman. "Refutation by the negative. Miss D. Yocum. Two minutes."

"I waive them," said Dora, primly. "I submit that the affirmative has not refuted the argument of the negative."

"Very well." With his gavel the chairman sharply tapped the desk before him, "The question is now before the house. 'Resolved, that Germany is both morally and legally justified in her invasion of Belgium.' All those in favour of the—"

But here there was an interruption of a kind never before witnessed during any proceedings of the Lumen Society. It came from neither of the debaters, who still remained standing at their desks until the vote settling their comparative merits in argument should be taken. The interruption was from the rear row of seats along the wall, where sat new members of the society, freshmen not upon the program for the evening. A loud voice was heard from this quarter, a loud but nasal voice, shrill as well as nasal, and full of a strange hot passion. "Mr. Chairman!" it cried. "Look-a-here, Mr. Chairman! Mr. Chairman, I demand to be heard! You gotta gimme my say, Mr. Chairman! I'm a-gunna have my *say*! You look-a-here, Mr. Chairman!"

Shocked by such a breach of order, and by the unseemly violence of the speaker, not only the chairman but everyone else looked there. A short, strong figure was on its feet, gesticulating fiercely; and the head belonging to it was a large one with too much curly black hair, a flat, swarthy face, shiny and not immaculately shaven; there was an impression of ill-chosen clothes, too much fat red lip, too much tooth, too much eyeball. Fred Mitchell, half-sorrowing, yet struggling to conceal tears of choked mirth over his roommate's late exhibition, recognized this violent interrupter as one Linski, a fellow freshman who sat next to him in one of his classes. "What's *that* cuss up to?" Fred wondered, and so did others. Linski showed them.

He pressed forward, shoving himself through the two rows in front of him till he emerged upon the green carpet of the open space, and as he came, he was cyclonic with words.

"You don't put no such stuff as this over, I tell you!" he shouted in his hot, nasal voice. "This here's a free country, and you call yourself a debating society, do you? Lemme tell you *I* belong to a debating society in Chicago, where I come from, and them fellas up there, they'd think they'd oughta be shot fer a fake like what you people are tryin' to put over, here, to-night. I come down here to git some more education, and pay fer it, too, in good hard money I've made sweatin' in a machine shop up there in Chicago; but if *this* is the kind of education I'm a-gunna git, I better go on back there. You call this a square debate, do you?"

He advanced toward the chairman's platform, shaking a frantic fist. "Well, if you do, you got another think comin', my capitalis' frien'! you went and give out the question whether it's right fer Choimuny to go through Belgium; and what do you do fer the Choimun side? You pick out this here big stiff"—he waved his passionate hand at the paralyzed Ramsey—"you pick out a boob like that for the Choimun side, a poor fish that gits stagefright so bad he don't know whether he's talkin' or dead; or else he fakes it; because he's a speaker so bum it looks more to me like he was faking. You get this big stiff to fake the Choimun side, and then you go and stick up a goil agains' him that's got brains and makes a pacifis' argument that wins the case agains' the Choimuns like cuttin' through hog lard! But you ain't a-gunna git away with it, mister! Lemme tell you right here and now, I may be a mix blood, but I got some Choimun in me with the rest what I got, and before you vote on this here question you gotta hear a few woids from somebody that can *talk!* This whole war is a capitalis' war, Belgium as much as Choimuny, and the United States is sellin' its soul to the capitalis' right now, I tell you, takin' sides agains' Choimuny. Orders fer explosives and ammanition and guns and Red Cross supplies is comin' into this country by the millions, and the capitalis' United States is fat already on the blood of the workers of Europe! Yes, it is, and I'll have my *say,* you boorjaw faker, and you can hammer your ole gavel to pieces at me!"

He had begun to shriek; moisture fell from his brow and his mouth; the scandalized society was on its feet, nervously into groups. Evidently the meeting was about to disintegrate. "I'll have my *say*!" the frenzied Linski screamed. "You try to put up this capitalis' trick and work a fake to carry over this debate agains' Choimuny, but you can't work it on *me,* lemme tell you! I'll have my *say!*"

The outraged chairman was wholly at a loss how to deal with the "unprecedented situation"—so he defined it, quite truthfully; and he continued to pound upon the desk, while other clamours began to rival Linski's; shouts of "Put him out!" "Order!" "Shut up, Freshman!" "Turn him over to the sophomores!"

"This meeting is *adjourned!*" bellowed the chairman, and there was a thronging toward the doors, while the frothing Linski asseverated: "I'm a-gunna git my say, I tell you! I'll have my say! I'll have my *say!*"

He had more than that, before the hour was over. A moment after he emerged from the building and came out, still hot, upon the cool, dark campus, he found himself the centre of a group of his own classmates whom he at first mistook for sophomores, such was their manner.

...As this group broke up, a few minutes later, a youth running to join it, scenting somewhat of interest, detained one of those who were departing.

"What's up? What was that squealing?"

"Oh, nothing. We just talked to that Linski. Nobody else touched him, but Ramsey Milholland gave him a *peach* of a punch on the snoot."

"Whoopee!"

Ramsey was laconic in response to inquiries upon this subject. When someone remarked: "You served him right for calling you a boob and a poor fish and so on before all the society, girls and all," Ramsey only said:

"That wasn't what I hit him for."

He declined to explain further.

CHAPTER XII

"The way I look at it, Ramsey," Fred Mitchell said, when they reached their apartment, whither the benevolent Colburn accompanied them, "the way I look at it, this Linski kind of paid you a compliment, after all, when he called you a fake. He must have thought you anyway *looked* as if you could make a better speech than you did. Oh, golly!"

And as Ramsey groaned, the jovial Mitchell gave himself up to the divan and the mirth. "Oh, oh, oh, *golly*!" he sputtered.

"Never you mind, Brother Milholland," Colburn said gently. "The Lumen is used to nervous beginners. I've seen dozens in my time, just like you; and some of 'em got to be first rate before they quit. Besides, this crazy Linski is all that anybody'll ever remember about to-night's meeting, anyhow. There never was any such outbreak as that in *my* time, and I guess there never was in the whole history of the society. We'll probably suspend him until he apologizes to the society—I'm on the board, and I'm in favour of it. Who is the bird, anyhow? He's in your class."

"I never saw him before," Ramsey responded from the deep chair, where he had moodily thrown himself; and, returning to his brooding upon his oratory. "Oh, murder!" he moaned.

"Well," said the senior, "you'll know him when you see him again. You put your mark on him where you can see it, all right!" He chuckled. "I suppose I really ought to have interfered in that, but I decided to do a little astronomical observation, about fifty feet away, for a few minutes. I'm 'way behind in my astronomy, anyhow. Do you know this Linski, Brother Mitchell?"

"I've talked to him a couple o' times on the campus," said Fred. "He's in one of my classes. He's about the oldest in our class, I guess—a lot older than us, anyhow. He's kind of an anarchist or something; can't talk more'n five minutes any time without gettin off some bug stuff about 'capitalism.' He said the course in political economy was all 'capitalism' and the prof was bought by Wall Street."

"Poor old Prof. Craig!" Colburn laughed. "He gets fifteen hundred a year."

"Yes; I'd heard that myself, and I told Linski, and he said he had an uncle workin' in a steel mill got twice that much; but it didn't make any difference, ole Craig was bought by Wall Street. He said 'capitalism' better look out; he and the foreign-born workmen were goin' to *take* this country some day, and that was one of the reasons he was after an education. He talked pretty strong pro-German, too—about the war in Europe—but I sort of thought that was more because he'd be pro-anything that he thought would help upset the United States than because he cared much about Germany."

"Yes," said Colburn, "that's how he sounded to-night. I guess there's plenty more like him in the cities, too. That reminds me, I'd better arrange a debate on immigration for the Lumen. We'll put Brother Milholland for the negative, this time."

Ramsey started violently. "See here—"

But the senior reassured him. "Just wanted to see you jump," he explained. "Don't fear; you've done your share."

"I should think I have!" Ramsey groaned.

"Yes, you won't be called on again this term. By the way," said Colburn, thoughtfully, "that was a clever girl you had against you to-night. I don't believe in pacificism much, myself, but she used it very niftily for her argument. Isn't she from your town, this Miss Yocum?"

Fred nodded.

"Well, she's a clever young thing," said the senior, still thoughtful. And he added: "Graceful girl, she is."

At this, the roommates looked at him with startled attention. Ramsey was so roused as to forget his troubles and sit forward in his chair.

"Yes," said the musing Colburn, "she's a mighty pretty girl."

"What!"

This exclamation was a simultaneous one; the astounded pair stared at him in blank incredulity.

"Why, don't you think so?" Colburn mildly inquired. "She seems to me very unusual looking."

"Well, yes," Fred assented, emphatically. "We're with you there!"

"Extraordinary eyes," continued Colburn. "Lovely figure,

too; altogether a strikingly pretty girl. Handsome, I should say, perhaps. Yes, 'handsome' rather than 'pretty'." He looked up from a brief reverie. "You fellows known her long?"

"You bet!" said Ramsey.

"She made a splendid impression on the Lumen," Colburn went on. "I don't remember that I ever saw a first appearance there that quite equalled it. She'll probably have a brilliant career in the society, and in the university, too. She must be a very fine sort of person." He deliberated within himself a few moments longer, then, realizing that his hosts and Brethren did not respond with any heartiness—or with anything at all—to the theme, he changed it, and asked them what they thought about the war in Europe.

They talked of the war rather drowsily for a while; it was an interesting but not an exciting topic: the thing they spoke of was so far away. It was in foreign countries where they had never been and had no acquaintances; and both the cause and the issue seemed to be in confusion, though evidently Germany had "started" the trouble. Only one thing emerged as absolutely clear and proved: there could be no disagreement about Germany's "dirty work," as Fred defined it, in violating Belgium. And this stirred Ramsey to declare with justice that "dirty work" had likewise been done upon himself by the official person, whoever he or she was, who had given him the German side of the evening's debate. After this moment of fervour, the conversation languished, and Brother Colburn rose to go.

"Well, I'm glad you gave that Linski a fine little punch, Brother Milholland," he said, at the door. "It won't do you any harm in the 'frat,' or with the Lumen either. And don't be discouraged about your debating. You'll learn. Anybody might have got rattled by having to argue against as clever and good-looking a girl as that!"

The roommates gave each other a look of serious puzzlement as the door closed. "Well, Brother Colburn is a mighty nice fellow," Fred said. "He's kind of funny, though."

Ramsey assented, and then, as the two prepared for bed, they entered into a further discussion of their senior friend. They liked him "all right," they said, but he certainly must be kind of queer, and they couldn't just see how he had "ever managed to get where he was" in the "frat" and the Lumen and the university.

CHAPTER XIII

Ramsey passed the slightly disfigured Linski on the campus next day without betraying any embarrassment or making a sign of recognition. Fred Mitchell told his roommate, chuckling, that Linski had sworn to "get" him, and, not knowing Fred's affiliations, had made him the confidant of his oath. Fred had given his blessing, he said, upon the enterprise, and advised Linski to use a brick. "He'll hit you on the head with it," said the light-hearted Fred, falling back upon this old joke. "Then you can catch it as it bounces off and throw it back at him."

However, Linski proved to be merely an episode, not only so far as Ramsey was concerned but in the Lumen and in the university as well. His suspension from the Lumen was for a year, and so cruel a punishment it proved for this born debater that he noisily declared he would found a debating society himself, and had a poster printed and distributed announcing the first meeting of "The Free Speech and Masses' Rights Council." Several town loafers attended the meeting, but the only person connected with the university who came was an oriental student, a Chinese youth of almost intrusive amiability. Linski made a fiery address, the townsmen loudly appluading his advocacy of an embargo on munitions and the distribution of everybody's "property," but the Chinaman, accustomed to see students so madly in earnest only when they were burlesquing, took the whole affair to be intended humour, and tittered politely without cessation—except at such times as he thought it proper to appear quite wrung with laughter. Then he would rock himself, clasp his mouth with both hands and splutter through his fingers. Linski accused him of being in the pay of "capital."

Next day the orator was unable to show himself upon the campus without causing demonstrations; whenever he was seen a file of quickly gathering students marched behind him chanting repeatedly and deafeningly in chorus: "Down with Wall Street! Hoch der Kaiser! Who loves Linski? Who, who, who? Hoo Lun! Who loves Linski? Who, who, who? Hoo Lun!"

Linski was disgusted, resigned from the university, and disappeared.

"Well, here it isn't mid-year Exams yet, and the good ole class of Nineteen-Eighteen's already lost a member," said Fred Mitchell. "I guess we can bear the break-up!"

"I guess so," Ramsey assented. "That Linski might just as well stayed here, though."

"Why?"

"He couldn't do any harm here. He'll prob'ly get more people to listen to him in cities where there's so many new immigrants and all such that don't know anything, comin' in all the time."

"Oh, well," said Fred. "What do *we* care what happens to Chicago! Come on, let's behave real wild, and go on over to the 'Teria and get us a couple egg sandwiches and sassprilly."

Ramsey was willing.

After the strain of the "mid-year Exams" in February, they lived a free-hearted life. They had settled into the ways of their world; they had grown used to it, and it had grown used to them; there was no longer any ignominy in being a freshman. They romped upon the campus and sometimes rioted harmlessly about the streets of the town. In the evenings they visited their fellows and Brethren and were visited in turn, and sometimes they looked so far ahead as to talk vaguely of their plans for professions or business— though to a freshman this concerned an almost unthinkably distant prospect. "I guess I'll go in with my father, in the wholesale drug business," said Fred. "My married brother already is in the firm, and I suppose they'll give me a show— send me out on the road a year or two first, maybe, to try me. Then I'm going to marry some little cutie and settle down. What you goin' to do, Ramsey? Go to Law School, and then come back and go in your father's office?"

"I don't know. Guess so."

It was always Fred who did most of the talking; Ramsey was quiet. Fred told the "frat seniors" that Ramsey was "developing a whole lot these days"; and he told Ramsey himself that he could see a "big change" in him, adding that the improvement was probably due to Ramsey's having passed through "terrible trials like that debate."

Ramsey kept to their rooms more than his comrade did, one reason for this domesticity being that he "had to study longer than Fred did, to keep up"; and another reason may have been a greater shyness than Fred possessed—if, indeed, Fred possessed any shyness at all. For Fred was a cheery spirit difficult to abash, and by the coming of spring knew all of the best-looking girl students in the place—knew them well enough, it appeared, to speak of them not merely by their first names but by abbreviations of these. He had become fashion's sprig, a "fusser" and butterfly, and he reproached his roommate for shunning the ladies.

"Well, the truth is, Fred," said Ramsey one day, responding darkly;—"well, you see the truth is, Fred, I've had a—a—I've had an experience—"

So, only, did he refer to Milla.

Fred said no more; and it was comprehended between them that the past need never be definitely referred to again, but that it stood between Ramsey and any entertainment to be obtained of the gentler but less trustworthy sex. And when other Brethren of the "frat" would have pressed Ramsey to join them in various frivolous enterprises concerning "co-eds," or to be shared by "co-eds," Fred thought it better to explain to them privately (all being sacred among Brethren) how Ramsey's life, so far as Girls went, had been toyed with by one now a Married Woman.

This created a great deal of respect for Ramsey. It became understood everywhere that he was a woman-hater.

CHAPTER XIV

That early spring of 1915 the two boys and their friends and Brethren talked more of the war than they had in the autumn, though the subject was not an all at absorbing one; for the trenches in Flanders and France were still of the immense, remote distance. By no stretch of imagination could these wet trenches be thought greatly to concern the "frat," the Lumen, or the university. Really important matters were the doings of the "Track Team," now training in the "Gym" and on the 'Varsity Field, and, more vital still, the prospects of the Nine. But in May there came a shock which changed things for a time.

The *Lusitania* brought to every American a revelation of what had lain so deep in his own heart that often he had not realized it was there. When the Germans hid in the sea and sent down the great merchant ship, with American babies and their mothers, and gallantly dying American gentlemen, there came a change even to girls and boys and professors, until then so preoccupied with their own little aloof world thousands of miles from the murder.

Fred Mitchell, ever volatile and generous, was one of those who went quite wild. No orator, he nevertheless made a frantic speech at the week's "frat meetings," cursing the Germans in the simple old English words that their performance had demonstrated to be applicable, and going on to demand that the fraternity prepare for its own share in the action of the country. "I don't care *how* insignificant we few fellows here to-night may seem," he cried; "we can do our little, and if everybody in this country's ready to do their own little, why, that'll be plenty! Brothers, don't you realize that all *over* the United States to-night the people are feeling just the way we are here? Millions and millions and millions of them! Wherever there's an American he's *with* us—and you bet your bottom dollar there are just a few more Americans in this country of ours than there are big-mouthed lobsters like that fellow Linski! I tell you, if Congress only gives the word, there could be an army of five million men in this country to-morrow, and those dirty baby-killin' dachs-hunds would hear a word or two from your Uncle Samuel! Brothers, I demand that something be done right here and now, and by us! I move we telegraph the Secretary of War to-night and offer him a regiment from this university to go over and help *hang* their damn Kaiser."

The motion was hotly seconded and instantly carried. Then followed a much flustered discussion of the form and phra-sing of the proposed telegram, but, after everything seemed to have been settled, someone ascertained by telephone that the telegraph company would not accept messages conta-ining words customarily defined as profane; so the telegram had to be rewritten. This led to further amendment, and it was finally decided to address the senators from that state, instead of the Secretary of War, and thus in a somewhat modified form the message was finally despatched.

Next day, news of what the "frat" had done made a great stir in the university; other "frats" sent telegrams, so did the "Barbarians," haters of the "frats" but joining them in this; while a small band of "German-American" students found it their duty to go before the faculty and report these "breaches of neutrality." They protested heavily, demanding the expulsion of the "breachers" as disloyal citizens, therefore unfit students, but suffered a disappointment; for the faculty itself had been sending telegrams of similar spirit, addressing not only the senators and congressmen of the state but the President of the United States. Flabbergasted, the "German-Americans" retired; they were confused and disgusted by this higher-up outbreak of unneutrality—it overwhelmed them that citizens of the United States should not remain neutral in the dispute between the United States and Germany. All day the campus was in ferment.

At twilight, Ramsey was walking meditatively on his way to dinner at the "frat house," across the campus from his apartment at Mrs. Meig's. Everybody was quiet now, both town and gown; the students were at their dinners and so were the burghers. Ramsey was late but did not quicken his thoughtful steps, which were those of one lost in reverie. He had forgotten that spring-time was all about him, and, with his head down, walked unregardful of the new gayeties flung forth upon the air by great clusters of flowering shrubs, just come into white blossom and lavender.

He was unconscious that somebody behind him, going the same way, came hastening to overtake him and called his name, "Ramsey! Ramsey Milholland!" Not until he had been called three times did he realize that he was being hailed—and in a girl's voice! By that time, the girl herself was beside him, and Ramsey halted, quite taken aback. The girl was Dora Yocum.

She was pale, a little breathless, and her eyes were bright and severe. "I want to speak to you," she said, quickly. "I want to ask you about something. Mr. Colburn and Fred Mitchell are the only people I know in your 'frat' except you, and I haven't seen either of them to-day, or I'd have asked one of them."

Most uncomfortably astonished, Ramsey took his hands out of his pockets, picked a leaf from a lilac bush beside the path, and put the stem of the leaf seriously into a corner of his mouth, before finding anything to say. "Well—well, all right," he finally responded. "I'll tell you—if it's anything I know about."

"You know about it," said Dora. "That is, you certainly do if you were at your 'frat' meeting last night. Were you?"

"Yes, I was there," Ramsey answered, wondering what in the world she wanted to know, though he supposed vaguely that it must be something about Colburn, whom he had several times seen walking with her. "Of course I couldn't tell you much," he added, with an afterthought. "You see, a good deal that goes on at a 'frat' meeting isn't supposed to be talked about."

"Yes," she said, smiling faintly, though with a satire that missed him. "I've been a member of a sorority since September, and I think I have an idea of what could be told or not told. Suppose we walk on, if you don't mind. My question needn't embarrass you."

Nevertheless, as they slowly went on together, Ramsey was embarrassed. He felt "queer." They had known each other so long; in a way had shared so much, sitting daily for years near each other and undergoing the same outward experiences; they had almost "grown up together," yet this was the first time they had ever talked together or walked together.

"Well—" he said. "If you want to ask anything it's all right for me to tell you—well, I just as soon, I guess."

"It has nothing to do with the secret proceedings of your 'frat'," said Dora, primly. "What I want to ask about has been talked of all over the place to-day. Everyone has been saying it was *your* 'frat' that sent the first telegram to members of the Government offering support in case of war with Germany. They say you didn't even wait until to-day, but sent off a message last night. What I wanted to ask you was whether this story is true or not?"

"Why, yes," said Ramsey, mildly. "That's what we did."

She uttered an exclamation, a sound of grief and of suspicion confirmed. "Ah! I was afraid so!"

"'Afraid so'? What's the matter?" he asked, and because she seemed excited and troubled, he found himself not quite so embarrassed as he had been at first; for some reason her agitation made him feel easier. "What was wrong about that?"

"Oh, it's all so shocking and wicked and mistaken!" she cried. "Even the faculty has been doing it, and half the other 'frats' and sororities! And it was yours that started it."

"Yes, we did," he said, throughly puzzled. "We're the oldest 'frat' here, and of course"—he chuckled modestly—"of course we think we're the best. Do you mean you believe we ought to've sat back and let somebody else start it?"

"Oh, *no*!" she answered, vehemently. "Nobody ought to have started it! That's the trouble; don't you see? If nobody had started it none of it might have happened. The rest mightn't have caught it. It mightn't have got into their heads. A war thought is the most contagious thought in the world; but if it can be kept from starting, it can be kept from being contagious. It's just when people have got into an emotional state, or a state of smouldering rage, that everybody ought to be so terribly careful not to think war thoughts or make war speeches—or send war telegrams! I thought—oh, I was so sure I'd convinced Mr. Colburn of all this, the last time we talked of it! He seemed to understand, and I was sure he agreed with me." She bit her lip. "He was only pretending—I see that now!"

"I guess he must 'a' been," said Ramsey, with admirable simplicity. "He didn't talk about anything like that last night. He was as much for it as anybody."

"I've no doubt!"

Ramsey made bold to look at her out of the side of his eye, and as she was gazing tensely forward he continued his observation for some time. She was obviously controlling agitation, almost controlling tears, which seemed to threaten her very wide-open eyes; for those now fully grown and noticeable eyewinkers of hers were subject to fluctuations indicating such a threat. She looked "hurt," and Ramsey was touched; there was something human about her, then, after all. And if he had put his feeling into words at the moment, he would have said that he guessed maybe he could stand this ole girl, for a few minutes sometimes, better than he'd always thought he could.

"Well," he said, "Colburn prob'ly wouldn't want to hurt your feelings or anything. Colburn—"

"He? He didn't! I haven't the faintest personal interest in what he did."

"Oh!" said Ramsey. "Well, excuse me; I thought prob'ly you were sore because he'd jollied you about this pacifist stuff, and then—"

"No!" she said, sharply. "I'm not thinking of his having

agreed with *me* and fooling *me* about it. He just wanted to make a pleasant impression on a girl, and said anything he thought would please her. I don't care whether he does things like that or not. What I care about is that the *principle* didn't reach him and that he mocked it! I don't care about a petty treachery to me, personally, but I—"

Fraternal loyalty could not quite brook this. "Brother Colburn is a perfectly honor'ble man," said Ramsey, solemnly. "He is one of the most honor'ble men in this—"

"Of course!" she cried. "Oh, can't I make you understand that I'm not condemning him for a little flattery to me? I don't care two straws for his showing that *I* didn't influence him. He doesn't interest me, please understand."

Ramsey was altogether perplexed. "Well, I don't see what makes you go for him so hard, then."

"I don't."

"But you said he was treach—"

"I don't *condemn* him for it," she insisted, despairingly. "Don't you see the difference? I'm not condemning anybody; I'm only lamenting.

"What about?

"About all of you that want *war*!"

"My golly!" Ramsey exclaimed. "You don't think those Dutchmen were right to drown babies and—"

"No! I think they were ghastly murderers! I think they were detestable and fiendish and monstrous and—"

"Well, then, my goodness! What do you want?"

"I don't want war!"

"You don't?"

"I want Christianity!" she cried. "I can't think of the Germans without hating them, and so to-day, when all the world is hating them, I keep myself from thinking of them as much as I can. Already half the world is full of war; you want to go to war to make things right, but it won't; it will only make more war!"

"Well, I—"

"Don't you see what you've done, you boys?" she said. "Don't you see what you've done with your absurd telegram? That started the rest; they thought they *all* had to send telegrams like that."

"Well, the faculty—"

"Even they mightn't have thought of it if it hadn't been for the first one. Vengeance is the most terrible thought; once you put it into people's minds that they ought to have it, it runs away with them."

"Well, it isn't mostly vengeance we're after, at all. There's a lot more to it than just getting even with—"

She did not heed him. "You're all blind! You don't see what you're doing; you don't even see what you've done to this peaceful place here. You've filled it full of thoughts of fury and killing and massacre—"

"Why, no," said Ramsey. "It was those Dutch did that to us;

and, besides, there's more to it than you—"

"No, there isn't," she interrupted. "It's just the old brutal spirit that nations inherit from the time they were only tribes; it's the tribe spirit, and an eye for an eye and a tooth for a tooth. It's those things and the love of fighting—men have always loved to fight. Civilization hasn't taken it out of them; men still have the brute in them that loves to fight!"

"I don't think so," said Ramsey. "Americans don't love to fight; I don't know about other countries, but we don't. Of course, here and there, there's some fellow that likes to hunt around for scrapes, but I never saw more than three or four in my life that acted that way. Of course a football team often has a scrapper or two on it, but that's different."

"No," she said. "I think you all really love to fight."

Ramsey was roused to become argumentative. "I don't see where you get the idea. Colburn isn't that way, and back at school there wasn't a single boy that was anything like that."

"What!" She stopped, and turned suddenly to face him.

"What's the matter?" he said, stopping, too. Something he said had startled her, evidently.

"How can you say such a thing?" she cried. "*You* love to fight!"

"Me?"

"You do! You love fighting. You always have loved fighting."

He was dumbfounded. "Why, I never had a fight in my life!"

She cried out in protest of such prevarication.

"Well, I never did," he insisted, mildly.

"Why, you had a fight about *me*!"

"No, I didn't."

"With Wesley Bender!"

Ramsey chuckled. "*That* wasn't a fight!"

"It wasn't?"

"Nothing like one. We were just guyin' him about—about gettin' slicked up, kind of, because he at in front of you; and he hit me with his book strap and I chased him off. Gracious, no; *that* wasn't a fight!"

"But you fought Linski only last fall."

Ramsey chuckled again. "That wasn't even as much like a fight as the one with Wesley. I just told this Linski I was goin' to give him a punch in the sn—I just told him to look out because I was goin' to hit him, and then I did it, and waited to see if he wanted to do anything about it, and he didn't. That's all there was to it, and it wasn't any more like fighting than—than feeding chickens is."

She laughed dolefully. "It seems to me rather more like it than that!"

"Well, it wasn't."

They had begun to walk on again, and Ramsey was aware that they had passed the "frat house," where his dinner was probably growing cold. He was aware of this, but not sharply or insistently. Curiously enough, he did not think about it. He had begun to find something pleasant in the odd interview, and in walking beside a girl, even though the girl was Dora Yocum. He made no attempt to account to himself for anything so peculiar.

For a while they went slowly together, not speaking, and without destination, though Ramsey vaguely took it for granted that Dora was going somewhere. But she wasn't. They emerged from the part of the small town closely built about the university and came out upon a bit of parked land overlooking the river; and here Dora's steps slowed to an indeterminate halt near a bench beneath a maple tree.

"I think I'll stay here a while," she said; and as he made no response, she asked, "Hadn't you better be going back to your 'frat house' for your dinner? I didn't mean for you to come out of your way with me; I only wanted to get an answer to my question. You'd better be running back."

"Well—"

He stood irresolute, not sure that he wanted his dinner just then. It would have amazed him to face the fact deliberately that perhaps he preferred being with Dora Yocum to eating. However, he faced no such fact, nor any fact, but lingered.

"Well—" he said again.

"You'd better go."

"I guess I can get my dinner pretty near any time. I don't—" He had a thought. "Did you—"

"Did I what?"

"Did you have your dinner before I met you?"

"No."

"Well, aren't you—"

She shook her head. "I don't want any."

"Why not?"

"I don't think people have very much appetite to-day and yesterday," she said, with the hint of a sad laugh, "all over America."

"No; I guess that's so."

"It's too terrible!" she said. "I can't sit and eat when I think of the *Lusitania*—of all those poor, poor people strangling in the water—"

"No; I guess nobody can eat much, if they think about that."

"And of what it's going to bring, if we let it," she went on. "As if this killing weren't enough, we want to add *our* killing! Oh, that's the most terrible thing of all—the thing it makes within us! Don't you understand?"

She turned to him appealingly, and he felt queerer than ever. Dusk had fallen. Where they stood, under the young-leaved maple tree, there was but a faint lingering of afterglow, and in this mystery her face glimmered wan and sweet; so that Ramsey, just then, was like one who discovers an old pan, used in the kitchen, to be made of chased silver.

"Well, I don't feel much like dinner right now," he said. "We—we could sit here awhile on this bench, prob'ly."

CHAPTER XV

Ramsey kept very few things from Fred Mitchell, and usually his confidences were immediate upon the occasion of them; but allowed several weeks to elapse before sketching for his roommate the outlines of this adventure.

"One thing that was kind o' funny about it, Fred," he said, "I didn't know what to call her."

Mr. Mitchell, stretched upon the window seat in their "study," and looking out over the town street below and the campus beyond the street, had already thought it tactful to ambush his profound amusement by turning upon his side, so that his face was toward the window and away from his companion. "What did you want to call her?" he inquired in a serious voice. "Names?"

"No. You know what I mean. I mean I had to just keep callin' her 'you'; and that gets kind of freaky when you're talkin' to anybody a good while like that. When she'd be lookin' away from me, and I'd want to start sayin' something to her, you know, why, I wouldn't know how to get started exactly, without callin' her something. A person doesn't want to be always startin' off with 'See here,' or things like that."

"I don't see why you let it trouble you," said Fred. "From

how you've always talked about her, you had a perfectly handy way to start off with anything you wanted to say to her."

"What with?"

"Why didn't you just say, 'Oh, you Teacher's Pet!' That would—"

"Get out! What I mean is, she called me 'Ramsey' without any bother; it seems funny I got stumped every time I started to say 'Dora.' Someway I couldn't land it, and it certainly would 'a' sounded crazy to call her 'Miss Yocum' after sittin' in the same room with her every day from the baby class clear on up through the end of high school. That *would* 'a' made me out an idiot!"

"What did you call her?" Fred asked.

"Just nothin' at all. I started to call her something or other a hundred times, I guess, and then I'd balk. I'd get all ready, and kind of make a sort of a sound, and then I'd have to quit."

"She may have thought you had a cold," said Fred, still keeping his back turned.

"I expect maybe she did—though I don't know; most of the time she didn't seem to notice me much, kind of."

"She didn't?"

"No. She was too upset, I guess, by what she was thinkin' about."

"But if it hadn't been for that," Fred suggested, "you mean

she'd have certainly paid more attention to who was sitting on the bench with her?"

"Get out! You know how it was. Everybody those few days thought we were goin' to have war, and she was just sure of it, and it upset her. Of course most people were a lot more upset by what those Dutchmen did to the *Lusitania* than by the idea of war; and she seemed to feel as broken up as anybody could be about the *Lusitania*, but what got her the worst was the notion of her country wantin' to fight, she said. She really was upset, too, Fred; there wasn't any puttin' on about it. I guess that ole girl certainly must have a good deal of feeling, because, doggoned, after we'd been sittin' there a while if she didn't have to get out her handkerchief! She kept her face turned away from me—just the same as you're doin' now to keep from laughin'—but honestly, she cried like somebody at a funeral. I felt like the darndest fool!"

"I'm not laughing," said Fred, but he did not prove it by turning so that his face could be seen. "What did she say?"

"Oh, she didn't say such an awful lot. She said one kind o' funny thing though: she said she was sorry she couldn't quite control herself, but if anybody had to see her cry she minded it less because it was an old schoolmate. What struck me so kind o' funny about that is—why, it looks as if she never knew the way I always hated her so."

"Yes," said Fred. "It wasn't flattering!"

"Well, sir, it *isn't*, kind of," Ramsey agreed, musingly. "It certainly isn't when you look at it that way."

"What did you say when she said that?" Fred asked.

"Nothin'. I started to, but I sort of balked again. Well, we kept on sitting there, and afterwhile she began to talk again and got kind of excited about how no war could do anything or anybody any good, and all war was wicked, no matter what it was about, and nothin' could be good that was founded on fear and hate, and every war that ever was fought was always founded on fear and hate. She said if the Germans wanted to fight us we ought to go to meet them and tell them we wouldn't fight."

"What did you say?"

"Nothin'. I kind o' started to—but what's the use? She's got that in her head. Besides, how are you goin' to argue about a thing with a person that's crying about it? I tell you, Fred, I guess we got to admit, after all, that ole girl certainly must have a lost of heart about her, anyway. There may not be much *fun* to her—though of course I wouldn't know hardly any way to tell about that—but there couldn't be hardly any doubt she's got a lot of feeling. Well, and then she went on and said old men made wars, but didn't fight; they left the fighting to the boys, and the suffering to the boy's mothers."

"Yes!" Fred exclaimed, and upon that he turned free of mirth for the moment. "That's the woman of it, I guess. Send the old men to do the fighting! For the matter of that, I guess my father'd about a thousand times go himself than see me and my brothers go; but Father's so fat he can't stoop! You got to be able to stoop to dig a trench, I guess! Well, suppose we sent our old men up against those Dutchmen; the Dutchmen would just kill the old men, and then come after the boys anyway, and the boys wouldn't be ready, and they'd get killed, too; and then there wouldn't be anybody but the Dutchmen left, and that'd be one fine world, wouldn't it?"

"Yes," said Ramsey. "Course I thought of that."

"Did you tell her?"

"No."

"What did you say?"

"Nothin'. I couldn't get started anyway, but, besides, what was the use? But she didn't want the old men to go; she didn't want anybody to go."

"What did she want the country to do?" Fred asked, impatiently.

"Just what it has been doin', I suppose. Just let things simmer down, and poke along, and let them do what they like to us."

"I guess so!" said Fred. "Then, afterwhile, when they get some free time on their hands, they'll come over and make it *really* interesting for us, because they know we won't do anything but talk. Yes, I guess the way things are settling down ought to suit Dora. There isn't goin' to be any war."

"She was pretty sure there was, though," Ramsey said, thoughtfully.

"Oh, of course she was then. We all thought so those few days."

"No. She said she thought it prob'ly wouldn't come right away, but now it was almost sure to come sometime. She said our telegrams and all the talk and so much feeling and everything showed her that the war thought that was always *in* people somewhere had been stirred up so it would go on and on. She said she knew from the way she felt herself about the *Lusitania* that a feeling like that in her would never be absolutely wiped out as long as she lived. But she said her other feeling about the horribleness of war taught her to keep the first feeling from breaking out, but with other people it wouldn't; and even if war didn't break out right then, it would always be ready to, all over the country, and sometime it would, though she was goin' to do her share to fight it, herself, as long as she could stand. She asked me wouldn't I be one of the ones to help her."

He paused, and after a moment Fred asked, "Well? What did you say to that?"

"Nothin'. I started to, but—"

Again Fred thought it tactful to turn and look out the window, while the agitation of his shoulders betrayed him.

"Go on and laugh! Well, so we stayed there quite a while, but before we left she got kind of more like everyday, you know, the way people do. It was half-past nine when we walked back in town, and I was commencin' to feel kind of hungry, so I asked her if she wasn't, and she sort of laughed and seemed to be ashamed of it, as if it were a disgrace or something, but she said she guessed she was; so I left her by that hedge of lilacs near the observatory and went on over to the 'Teria and the fruit store, and got some stuffed eggs and olives and half-a-dozen peanut butter sandwiches and a box o' strawberries—kind of girl-food, you know—and went on back there, and we ate the stuff up. So then she said she was afraid she'd taken me away from my dinner and made me a lot of trouble, and so on, and she was sorry, and she told me good-night—"

"What did you say then?"

"Noth— Oh, shut up! So then she skipped out to her Dorm, and I came on home."

"When did you see her next, Ramsey?"

"I haven't seen her next," said Ramsey. "I haven't seen her at all—not to speak to. I saw her on Main Street twice since then, but both times she was with some other girls, and they were across the street, and I couldn't tell if she was lookin' at me—I kind of thought not—so I thought it might look sort o' nutty to bow to her if she wasn't, so I didn't."

"And you didn't tell her you wouldn't be one of the ones to help her with her pacifism and anti-war stuff and all that?"

"No. I started to, but— Shut up!"

Fred sat up, giggling. "So she thinks you *will* help her. You didn't say anything at all, and she must think that means she converted you. Why didn't you speak up?"

"Well, *I* wouldn't argue with her," said Ramsey. Then, after a silence, he seemed to be in need of sympathetic comprehension. "It *was* kind o' funny, though, wasn't it?" he said, appealingly.

"What was?"

"The whole business."

"What 'whole bus'—"

"Oh, get out! Her stoppin' me, and me goin' pokin' along with her, and her—well, her crying and everything, and me being around with her while she felt so upset, I mean. It seems—well, it does seem kind o' funny to me."

"Why does it?" Fred inquired, preserving his gravity. "Why should it seem funny to you?"

"I don't mean funny like something's funny you laugh at," Ramsey explained laboriously. "I mean funny like something that's out of the way, and you wonder how it ever happened to happen. I mean it seems funny I'd ever be sittin' there on a bench with that ole girl I never spoke to in my life or had anything to do with, and talkin' about the United States goin' to war. What we were talkin' about, why, that seems just as funny as the rest of it. Lookin' back to our class picnic, f'r instance, second year of high school, that day I jumped in the creek after—Well, you know, it was when I started makin' a fool of myself over a girl. Thank goodness, I got *that* out o' my system; it makes me just sick to look back on those days and think of the fool things I did, and all I thought about that girl. Why, she—Well, I've got old enough to see now she was just about as ordinary a girl as there ever was, and if I saw her now I wouldn't even think she was pretty; I'd prob'ly think she was sort of loud-lookin'. Well, what's passed is past, and it isn't either here nor there. What I started to say was this: that the way it begins to look to me, it looks as if nobody can tell in this life a darn thing about what's goin' to happen, and the things that do happen are the very ones you'd swear were the last that could. I mean—you look back to that day of the picnic—my! but I was a rube then—well, I mean you look back to that day, and what do you suppose I'd have thought then if somebody'd told me the time would ever come when I'd be 'way off here at college sittin' on a bench with Dora Yocum—with *Dora Yocum*, in the first place— and her crying, and both of us talking about the United States goin' to war with Germany! Don't it seem pretty funny to you, Fred, too?"

"But as near as I can make out," Fred said, "that isn't what happened."

"Why isn't it?"

"You say 'and both us talking' and so on. As near as I can make out, *you* didn't say anything at all."

"Well, I didn't—much," Ramsey admitted, and returned to his point with almost pathetic persistence. "But doesn't it seem kind o' funny to you, Fred?"

"Well, I don't know."

"It does to me," Ramsey insisted. "It certainly does to me."

"Yes," said Fred cruelly. "I've noticed you said so, but it don't look any funnier than you do when you say it."

Suddenly he sent forth a startling shout. "*Wow!* You're as red as a blushing beet."

"I am not!"

"Y'are!" shouted Fred. "Wow! The ole woman-hater's got the flushes! Oh, look at the pretty posy!"

And, jumping down from the window seat, he began to dance round his much perturbed comrade, bellowing. Ramsey bore with him for a moment, then sprang upon him; they wrestled vigorously, broke a chair, and went to the floor with a crash that gave the chandelier in Mrs. Meig's parlour, below, an attack of jingles.

"You let me up!" Fred gasped.

"You take your solemn oath to shut up? You goin' to swear it?"

"All right. I give my solemn oath," said Fred; and they rose, arranging their tousled attire.

"Well," said Fred, "when you goin' to call on her?"

"You look here!" Ramsey approached him dangerously. "You just gave me your sol—"

"I beg!" Fred cried, retreating. "I mean, aside from all that, why, I just thought maybe after such an evening you'd feel as a gentleman you ought to go and ask about her health."

"Now, see here—"

"No, I mean it; you ought to," Fred insisted, earnestly, and as his roommate glared at him with complete suspicion, he added, in explanation. "You ought to go next Caller's Night, and send in your card, and say you felt you ought to ask if she'd suffered any from the night air. Even if you couldn't manage to say that, you ought to start to say it, anyhow, because you— Keep off o' me! I'm only tryin' to do you a good turn, ain't I?"

"You save your good turns for yourself," Ramsey growled, still advancing upon him.

But the insidious Mitchell, evading him, fled to the other end of the room, picked up his cap, and changed his manner. "Come on, ole bag o' beans, let's be on our way to the 'frat house'; it's time. We'll call this all off."

"You better!" Ramsey warned him; and they trotted out together.

But as they went along, Fred took Ramsey's arm confidentially, and said, "Now, honestly, Ram, ole man, when *are* you goin' to—"

Ramsey was still red. "You look here! Just say one

more word—"

"Oh, *no*," Fred expostulated. "I mean *seriously*, Ramsey. Honestly, I mean seriously. Aren't you seriously goin' to call on her some Caller's Night?"

"No, I'm not!"

"But why not?"

"Because I don't want to."

"Well, seriously, Ramsey, there's only one Caller's Night before vacation, and so I suppose it hardly will be worth while; but I expect you'll see quite a little of her at home this summer?"

"No, I won't. I won't see her at all. She isn't goin' to be home this summer, and I wouldn't see anything of her if she was."

"Where's she goin' to be."

"In Chicago."

"She is?" said Fred, slyly. "When'd she tell you?"

Ramsey turned on him. "You look out! She didn't tell me. I just happened to see in the *Bulletin* she's signed up with some other girls to go and do settlement work in Chicago. Anybody could see it. It was printed out plain. You could have seen it just as well as I could, if you'd read the *Bulletin*."

"Oh," said Fred.

"Now look here—"

"Good heavens! Can't I even say 'oh'?"

"It depends on the way you say it."

"I'll be careful," Fred assured him, earnestly. "I really and honestly don't mean to get you excited about all this, Ramsey. I can see myself you haven't changed from your old opinion of Dora Yocum a bit. I was only tryin' to get a little rise out of you for a minute, because of course, seriously, why, I can see you hate her just the same as you always did."

"Yes," said Ramsey, disarmed and guileless in the face of diplomacy. "I only told you about all this, Fred, because it seemed—well, it seemed so kind o' funny to me."

Fred affected not to hear. "What did you say, Ramsey?"

Ramsey looked vaguely disturbed. "I said—why, I said it all seemed kind o'—" He paused, then repeated plaintively: "Well, to me, it all seemed kind o'—kind o' funny."

"What did?" Fred inquired, but as he glanced in seeming naivete at his companion, something he saw in the latter's eye warned him, and suddenly Fred thought it would be better to run.

Ramsey chased him all the way to the "frat house."

CHAPTER XVI

Ramsey was not quite athlete enough for any of the 'varsity teams; neither was he an antagonist safely encountered, whether in play or in earnest, and during the next few days he taught Fred Mitchell to be cautious. The chaffer learned that his own agility could not save him from Ramsey, and so found it wiser to contain an effervescence which sometimes threatened to burst him. Ramsey as a victim was a continuous temptation, he was so good-natured and yet so furious.

After Commencement, when the roommates had gone home, Mr. Mitchell's caution extended over the long sunshiny months of summer vacation; he broke it but once and then in well-advised safety, for the occasion was semi-public. The two were out for a stroll on a July Sunday afternoon; and up and down the street young couples lolled along, young families and baby carriages straggled to and from the houses of older relatives, and the rest of the world of that growing city was rocking and fanning itself on its front veranda.

"Here's a right pretty place, isn't it, Ramsey? don't you think?" Fred remarked innocently, as they were passing a lawn of short-clipped, bright green grass before a genial-looking house, fresh in white paint and cool in green-and-white awnings. A broad veranda, well populated just now, crossed the front of the house; fine trees helped the awnings to give comfort against the sun; and Fred's remark was warranted. Nevertheless, he fell under the suspicion of his companion, who had begun to evince some nervousness before Fred spoke.

"What place do you mean?"

"The Yocum place," said Mr. Mitchell. "I hear the old gentleman's mighty prosperous these days. They keep things up to the mark, don't they, Ramsey?"

"I don't know whether they do or whether they don't," Ramsey returned shortly.

Fred appeared to muse regretfully. "It looks kind of *empty* now, though," he said, "with only Mr. and Mrs. Yocum and their three married daughters, and eight or nine children on the front porch!"

"You wait till I get you where they can't see us!" Ramsey warned him, fiercely.

"You can't do it!" said Fred, manifesting triumph. "We'll both stop right here in plain sight of the whole Yocum family connection till you promise not to touch me."

And he halted, leaning back implacably against the Yocum's iron fence. Ramsey was scandalized.

"Come on!" he said, hoarsely. "Don't stop *here*!"

"I will, and if you go on alone I'll yell at you. You got to stand right here with all of 'em lookin' at you until—"

"I promise! My heavens, come *on*!"

Fred consented to end the moment of agony; and for the rest of the summer found it impossible to persuade Ramsey to pass that house in his company. "I won't do it!" Ramsey told him. "Your word of honour means nothin' to me; you're liable to do anything that comes into your head, and I'm gettin' old enough to not get a reputation for bein' seen with people that act the idiot on the public streets. No, sir; we'll walk around the block—at least, we will if you're goin' with *me*!"

And to Fred's delight, though he concealed it, they would make this detour.

The evening after their return to the university both were busy with their trunks and various orderings and disorderings of their apartment, but Fred several times expressed surprise that his roommate should be content to remain at home; and finally Ramsey comprehended the implications. Mrs. Meigs's chandelier immediately jingled with the shock of another crash upon the floor above.

"You let me up!" Fred commanded thickly, his voice muffled by the pile of flannels, sweaters, underwear, and raincoats wherein his head was being forced to burrow. "You let me up, darn you! *I* didn't say anything." And upon his release he complained that the attack was unprovoked. "I didn't say anything on earth to even hint you might want to go out and look around to see if anybody in particular had got back to college yet. I didn't even mention the *name* of Dora Yo— Keep off o' me! My goodness, but you are sensitive!"

As a matter of fact, neither of them saw Dora until the first meeting of the Lumen, whither they went as sophomores to take their pleasure in the agony of freshmen debaters. Ramsey was now able to attend the Lumen, not with complacence but at least without shuddering over the recollection of his own spectacular first appearance there. He had made subsequent appearances, far from brilliant yet not disgraceful, and as a spectator, at least, he usually felt rather at his ease in the place. It cannot be asserted, however, that he appeared entirely at his ease this evening after he had read the "Programme" chalked upon the large easel blackboard beside the chairman's desk. Three "Freshmen Debates" were announced, and a "Sophomore Oration," this last being followed by the name, "D. Yocum, '18." Ramsey made immediate and conspicuous efforts to avoid sitting next to his roommate, but was not so adroit as to be successful. However, Fred was merciful: the fluctuations of his friend's complexion were an inspiration more to pity than to badinage.

The three debates all concerned the "Causes of the War in Europe," and honours appeared to rest with a small and stout, stolidly "pro-German" girl debater, who had brought with her and translated at sight absa-loot proofs (so she called them), printed in German, that Germany had been attacked by Belgium at the low instigation of the envious English. Everybody knew it wasn't true; but she made an impression and established herself as a debater, especially as her opponent was quite confounded by her introduction of printed matter.

When the debates and the verdicts were concluded, the orator appeared, and Fred's compassion extended itself so far that he even refrained from looking inquisitively at the boy in the seat next to his; but he made one side wager, mentally—that if Ramsey had consented to be thoroughly confidential just then, he would have confessed to feeling kind o' funny.

Dora was charmingly dressed, and she was pale; but those notable eyelashes of hers were all the more notable against her pallor. And as she spoke with fire, it was natural that her colour should come back quite flamingly and that her eyes should flash in shelter of the lashes. "The Christian Spirit and Internationalism" was her subject, yet she showed no meek sample of a Christian Spirit herself when she came to attacking war-makers generally, as well as all those "half-developed tribesmen," and "victims of herd instinct" who believed that war might ever be justified under any circumstances of atrocity. She was eloquent truly, and a picture of grace and girlish dignity, even when she was most vigorous. Nothing could have been more militant than her denunciation of militancy.

"She's an actual wonder," Fred said, when the two had got back to Mrs. Meigs's, afterward. "Don't you look at me like that: I'm talkin' about her as a public character, and there's nothin' personal about it. You let me alone."

Ramsey was not clear as to his duty. "Well—"

"If any person makes a public speech," Fred protested, "I got a perfect right to discuss 'em, no matter what you think of 'em"—and he added hastily—"or *don't* think of 'em!"

"Look here—"

"Good heavens!" Fred exclaimed. "You aren't expecting to interfere with me if I say anything about that little fat Werder girl that argued for Germany, are you? Or any of the other speakers? I got a right to talk about 'em just as public speakers, haven't I? Well, what I say is: Dora Yocum as an orator is just an actual perfect wonder. Got any objections?"

"N-no."

"All right then." Fred settled himself upon the window seat

with a pipe, and proceeded, "There's something about her, when she stands there, she stands so straight and knows just what she's up to, and everything, why, there's something about her makes the cold chills go down your spine—I mean *my* spine, not yours particularly! You sit down—I mean *anybody's* spine, doggone it!" And as Ramsey increased the manifestations of his suspicions, lifting a tennis racket over the prostrate figure, "Oh, murder," Fred said, resignedly. "All right, we'll change the subject. That fat little Werder cutie made out a pretty good case for Germany, didn't she?"

Ramsey tossed the racket away, disposed himself in an easy chair with his feet upon the table, and presently chuckled. "You remember the time I had the fuss with Wesley Bender, back in the ole school days?"

"Yep."

"All the flubdub this Werder girl got off to-night puts me in mind of the way I talked that day. I can remember it as well as anything! Wesley kept yelpin' that whoever mentioned a lady's name in a public place was a pup, and of course I didn't want to hit him for that; a boy's got a reg'lar instinct for tryin' to make out he's on the right side in a scrap, and he'll always try to do something, or say something, or he'll get the other boy to say someting to make it look as if the other boy was in the wrong and began the trouble. So I told poor ole Wes that my father spoke my mother's name in a public place whenever he wanted to, and I dared him to say my father was a pup. And all so on. A boy startin' up a scrap, why, half the time he'll drag his father and mother if there's any chance to do it. He'll fix up some way so he can say, 'Well, that's just the same as if you called my father and mother a fool,' or something like that. Then, afterward, he can claim he was scrappin' because he had to defend his father and mother, and of course he'll more than half believe it himself.

"Well, you take a Government—it's only just some *men*, the way I see it, and if they're goin' to start some big trouble like this war, why, of course they'll play just about the same ole boy trick, because it's instinct to do it, just the same for a man as it is for a boy—or else the principle's just the same, or something. Well, anyhow, if you want to know who started a scrap and worked it up, you got to forget all the *talk* there is about it, and all what each side *says*, and just look at two things: Who was fixed for it first, or thought they were, and who hit first? When you get the answer to those two questions everything's settled about all this being 'attacked' business. Both sides, just the same as boys, they'll both claim they *had* to fight; but if you want to know which one *did* have to, why forget all the arguing and don't take your eye off just what *happened*. As near as I can make out, this war began with Germany and Austria startin' in to wipe out two little countries; Austria began shootin' up Serbia, and Germany began shootin' up Belgium. I don't need to notice any more than that, myself—all the Werder girls in the country can debate their heads off, they can't change what happened and they can't excuse it, either."

He was silent, appearing to feel that he had concluded conclusively, and the young gentleman on the window seat, after staring at him for several moments of genuine thoughtfulness, was gracious enough to observe, "Well, ole Ram, you may be a little slow in class, but when you think things out with yourself you do show signs of something pretty near like real horse-sense sometimes. Why don't you ever say anything like that to—to some of your pacifist friends?"

"What do you mean? Who you talkin' about? Whose 'pacifist friends'?"

"See here!" Fred exclaimed, as Ramsey seemed about to rise. "You keep sitting just where you are, and don't look at me out of the side of your eye like that—pretendin' you're a bad horse. I'm *really* serious now, and you listen to me. I don't think argufying and debating like that little Fraulein Werder's does much harm. She's a right nifty young rolypoly, by the way, though you didn't notice, of course."

"Why didn't I?" Ramsey demanded, sharply. "Why didn't I notice?"

"Oh, nothing. But, as I was saying, I don't think that sort of talk does much harm: everybody knows it goes on among the pro-Germans, and it's all hot air, anyhow. But I think Linski's sort of talk does do harm, prob'ly among people that don't know much; and what's more, I think Dora Yocum's does some, too. Well, you hit Linski in the snoot, so what are you—Sit still! My lord! You don't think I'm askin' you to go and hit Dora, do you? I mean: Aren't you ever goin' to talk to her about it and tell her what's what?"

"Oh, you go on to bed!"

"No, I'm in earnest," Fred urged. "Honestly, aren't you ever goin' to?"

"How could I do anything like that?" Ramsey demanded explosively. "I never see her—to speak to, that is. I prob'ly won't happen to have another talk with her, or anything, all the time we're in college."

"No," Fred admitted, "I suppose not. Of course, if you did, then you would give her quite a talking-to, just the way you did the other time, wouldn't you?" But upon that, another resumption of physical violence put an end to the conversation.

CHAPTER XVII

Throughout the term Ramsey's calculation of probabilities against the happening of another interview with Dora seemed to be well founded, but at the beginning of the second "semester" he found her to be a fellow member of a class in biology. More than that, this class had every week a two-hour session in the botanical laboratory, where the structure of plants was studied under microscopic dissection. The students worked in pairs, a special family of plants being assigned to each couple; and the instructor selected the couples with an eye to combinations of the quick with the slow. D. Yocum and R. Milholland (the latter in a strange state of mind and complexion) were given two chairs, but only one desk and one microscope. Their conversation was strictly botanical.

Thenceforth it became the most pressing care of Ramsey's life to prevent his roommate from learning that there was any conversation at all, even botanical. Fortunately, Fred was not taking the biological courses, though he appeared to be taking the sentimental ones with an astonishing thoroughness; and sometimes, to Fred's hilarious delight, Ramsey attempted to turn the tables and rally him upon whatever last affair seemed to be engaging his fancy. The old Victorian and pre-Victorian *blague* word "petticoat" had been revived in Fred's vocabulary, and in others, as "skirt." The lightsome sprig was hourly to be seen, even when university rulings forbade, dilly-dallying giddily along the campus paths or the town sidewalks with some new and pretty Skirt. And when Ramsey tried to fluster him about such a matter Fred would profess his ardent love for the new lady in shouts and impromptu song. Nothing could be done to him, and Ramsey, utterly unable to defend his own sensibilities in like manner, had always to retire in bafflement. Sometimes he would ponder upon the question thus suggested: Why couldn't he do this sort of thing, since Fred could? But he never discovered a satisfying answer.

Ramsey's watchfulness was so careful (lest he make some impulsive admission in regard to the botanical laboratory, for instance) that Mr. Mitchell's curiosity gradually became almost quiescent; but there arrived a day in February when it was piqued into the liveliest activity. It was Sunday, and Fred, dressing with a fastidiousness ever his daily habit, noticed that Ramsey was exhibiting an unusual perplexity about neckties.

"Keep the black one on," Fred said, volunteering the suggestion, as Ramsey muttered fiercely at a mirror. "It's in better taste for church, anyhow. You're going to church, aren't you?"

"Yes. Are you?"

"No. I've got a luncheon engagement."

"Well, you could go to church first, couldn't you? You better; you've got a lot of church absences against you."

"Then one more won't hurt. No church in mine this morning, thanks! G'by, ole sox; see you at the 'frat house' for dinner."

He went forth, whistling syncopations, and began a brisk trudge into the open country. There was a professor's daughter who also was not going to church that morning; and she lived a little more than three miles beyond the outskirts of the town. Unfortunately, as the weather was threatening, all others of her family abandoned the idea of church that day, and Fred found her before a cozy fire, but surrounded by parents, little brothers, and big sisters. The professor was talkative; Fred's mind might have been greatly improved, but with a window in range he preferred a melancholy contemplation of the snow, which had begun to fall in quantity. The professor talked until luncheon, throughout luncheon, and was well under way to fill the whole afternoon with talk, when Fred, repenting all the errors of his life, got up to go.

Heartily urged to remain, for there was now something just under a blizzard developing, he said No; he had a great deal of "cirriculum work" to get done before the morrow, and passed from the sound of the professor's hospitable voice and into the storm. He had a tedious struggle against the wind and thickening snow, but finally came in sight of the town, not long before dark. Here the road led down into a depression, and, lifting his head as he began the slight ascent on the other side, Fred was aware of two figures outlined upon the low ridge before him. They were dimmed by the driving snow and their backs were toward him, but he recognized them with perfect assurance. They were Dora Yocum and Ramsey Milholland.

They were walking so slowly that their advance was almost imperceptible, but it could be seen that Dora was talking with great animation; and she was a graceful thing, thus gesticulating, in her long, slim fur coat with the white snow frosting her brown fur cap. Ramsey had his hands deep in his overcoat pockets and his manner was wholly that of an audience.

Fred murmured to himself, "'What did you say to her?' 'Nothin'. I started to, but'—" Then he put on a burst of speed and passed them, sweeping off his hat with operatic deference, yet hurrying by as if fearful of being thought a killjoy if he lingered. He went to the "frat house," found no one downstairs, and established himself in a red leather chair to smoke and ruminate merrily by a great fire in the hall.

Half an hour later Ramsey entered, stamped off the snow, hung up his hat and coat, and sat himself down defiantly in the red leather chair on the other side of the fireplace.

"Well, go on," he said. "Commence!"

"Not at all!" Fred returned, amiably. "Fine spring weather to-day. Lovely to see all the flowers and the birds as we go a-strolling by. The little bobolinks—"

"You look here! That's the only walk I ever took with her in my life. I mean by—by asking her and her saying she would and so forth. That other time just sort of happened, and you know it. Well, the weather wasn't just the best in the world, maybe, but she's an awful conscientious girl and once she makes an engagement—"

"Why, of course," Fred finished for him, "She'd be too pious to break it just on account of a mere little blizzard or anything. Wonder how the weather will be next Sunday?"

"I don't know and I don't care," said Ramsey. "You don't suppose I asked her to go *again*, do you?"

"Why not?"

"Well, for one thing, you don't suppose I want her to think I'm a perfect fool, do you?"

Booth Tarkington

Fred mused a moment or two, looking at the fire. "What was the lecture?" he asked, mildly.

"What lecture?"

"She seemed to me to be—"

"That wasn't lecturing; she was just—"

"Just what?"

"Well; she thinks war for the United States is coming closer and closer—"

"But it isn't."

"Well, she thinks so, anyhow," said Ramsey, "and she's all broken up about it. Of course she thinks we oughtn't to fight and she's trying to get everybody else she can to keep working against it. She isn't goin' home again next summer, she's goin' back to that settlement work in Chicago and work there among those people against our goin' to war; and here in college she wants to get everybody she can to talk against it, and—"

"What did you say?" Fred asked, and himself supplied the reply: "Nothin'. I started to, but—"

Ramsey got up. "Now look here! You know the 'frat' passed a rule that if we broke any more furniture in this house with our scrappin' we'd both be fined the cost of repairs and five dollars apiece. Well, I can afford five dollars this month better than you can, and—"

"I take it back!" Fred interposed, hastily. "But you just listen to me; you look out—letting her think you're on her side like that."

"I don't—"

"You *don't?*"

Ramsey looked dogged. "I'm not goin' around always arguin' about everything when arguin' would just hurt people's feelings about something they're all excited about, and wouldn't do a bit o' good in the world—and you know yourself just *talk* hardly ever settles anything—so I don't—"

"Aha!" Fred cried. "I thought so! Now you listen to me—"

"I won't. I—"

But at this moment they were interrupted. Someone slyly opened the door, and a snowball deftly thrown from without caught Ramsey upon the back of the neck and head, where it flattened and displayed itself as an ornamental star. Shouting fiercely, both boys sprang up, ran to the door, were caught there in a barrage of snowballs, ducked through it in spite of all damage, charged upon a dozen besweatered figures awaiting them and began a mad battle in the blizzard. Some of their opponents treacherously joined them, and turned upon the ambushers.

In the dusk the merry conflict waged up and down the snow-covered lawn, and the combatants threw and threw, or surged back and forth, or clenched and toppled over into snow banks, yet all coming to chant an extemporized battle-cry in chorus, even as they fought the most wildly.

"Who? Who? Who?" they chanted. "Who? Who? *Who* says there ain't goin' to be no war?"

CHAPTER XVIII

So everywhere over the country, that winter of 1916, there were light-hearted boys skylarking—at college, or on the farms; and in the towns the young machinists snowballed one another as they came from the shops; while on this Sunday of the "frat" snow fight probably several hundreds of thousands of youthful bachelors, between the two oceans, went walking, like Ramsey, each with a girl who could forget the weather. Yet boys of nineteen and in the twenties were not light-hearted all the time that winter and that spring and that summer. Most of them knew long, thoughtful moments, as Ramsey did, when they seemed to be thinking not of girls or work or play—nor of anything around them, but of some more vital matter or prospect. And at such times they were grave, but not ungentle.

For the long strain was on the country; underneath all its outward seeming of things going on as usual there shook a deep vibration, like the air trembling to vast organ pipes in diapasons too profound to reach the ear as sound: one felt, not heard, thunder in the ground under one's feet. The succession of diplomatic Notes came to an end after the torpedoing of the *Sussex*; and at last the tricky ruling Germans in Berlin gave their word to murder no more, and people said, "This means peace for America, and all is well for us," but everybody knew in his heart that nothing was well for us, that there was no peace.

They said "All is well," while that thunder in the ground never ceased—it grew deeper and heavier till all America shook with it and it became slowly audible as the voice of the old American soil wherein lay those who had defended it aforetime, a soil that bred those who would defend it again, for it was theirs; and the meaning of it—Life, Liberty, and the Pursuit of Happiness—was theirs, and theirs to defend. And they knew they would defend it, and that more than the glory of a Nation was at stake. The Freedom of Man was at stake. So, gradually, the sacred thunder reached the ears of the young men and gave them those deep moments that came to them whether they sat in the classroom or the counting-room, or walked with the plow, or stood to the machine, or behind the ribbon counter. Thus the thunder shook them and tried them and slowly came into their lives and changed everything for them.

Hate of the Germans was not bred; but a contempt for what Germany had shown in lieu of a national heart; a contempt as mighty and profound as the resolve that the German way and the German will should prevail in America, nor in any country of the world that would be free. And when the German Kaiser laid his command upon America, that no American should take his ship upon the free seas, death being the penalty for any who disobeyed, then the German Kaiser got his answer, not only to this new law he had made for us, but to many other thoughts of his. Yet the answer was for some time delayed.

There was a bitter Sunday, and its bitterness went every-where, to every place in the whole world that held high and generous hearts. Its bitterness came to the special meeting in the "Frat hall," where there were hearts, indeed, of that right sort, and one of them became vocal in its bitterness. This was the heart of Fred Mitchell, who was now an authority, being president of the Junior Class, chairman of the Prom Committee, and other things pleasant to be and to live for at his age.

"For me, Brothers," he said, "I'd think I'd a great deal rather have been shot through the head than heard the news from Washington to-day! I tell you, I've spent the meanest afternoon I ever did in my life, and I guess it's been pretty much the same with all of us. The worst of it is, it looks as though there isn't a thing in the world we can do. The country's been betrayed by a few blatherskites and bone-heads that had the power to do it, and all we can do we've just got to stand it. But there's some Americans that aren't just standing it, and I want to tell you a lot of 'em are men from the universities, just like us. They're *over there* right now; they haven't said much—they just packed up and went. They're flying for France and for England and for Canada; they're fighting under every flag on the right side of the Western Front; and they're driving ambulances at Verdun and ammunition trucks at the Somme. Well, there's going to be a lot more American boys on all these jobs mighty soon, on account of what those men did in Congress to-day. If they won't give us a chance to do something under our own flag, then we'll have to go and do it under some other flag; and I want to tell you I'm one that's going to *go!* I'll stick it out in college up to Easter, and then if there's still no chance to go under the Stars and Stripes I'll maybe have to go under the flag my great-great-grandfather fought against in 1776, but, anyhow, I'll *go!*"

It was in speaking to Ramsey of this declaration that Dora said Fred was a "dangerous firebrand." They were taking another February walk, but the February was February, 1917; and the day was dry and sunny. "It's just about a year ago," she said.

"What is?" Ramsey asked.

"That first time we went walking. Don't you remember?"

"Oh, *that* day? Yes, I remember it was snowing."

"And so cold and blowy!" she added. "It seems a long time ago. I like walking with you, Ramsey. You're so quiet and solid—I've always felt I could talk to you just anyhow I pleased, and you wouldn't mind. I'll miss these walks with you when we're out of college."

He chuckled. "That's funny!"

"Why?"

"Because we've only taken four besides this: two last year, and another week before last, and another last week. This is only the fifth."

"Good gracious! Is that all? It seemed to me we'd gone ever so often!" She laughed. "I'm afraid you won't think that seems much as if I'd liked going, but I really have. And, by the way, you've never called on me at all. Perhaps it's because I've forgotten to ask you."

"Oh, no," Ramsey said, and scuffed his shoes on the path, presently explaining rather huskily that he "never *was* much of a caller"; and he added, "or anything."

"Well, you must come if you ever care to," she said, with a big-sister graciousness. "The Dorm chaperon sits there, of course, but ours is a jolly one and you'd like her. You've probably met her—Mrs. Hustings?—when you've called on other girls at our old shop."

"No," said Ramsey. "I never was much of a—" He paused, fearing that he might be repeating himself, and too hastily amended his intention. "I never liked any girl enough to go and call on her."

"Ramsey Milholland!" she cried. "Why, when we were in school half the room used to be talking about how you and that pretty Milla—"

"No, no!" Ramsey protested, again too hurriedly. "I never called on her. We just went walking."

A moment later his colour suddenly became fiery. "I don't mean—I mean—" he stammered. "It was walking, of course —I mean we did go out walking but it wasn't walking like— like this." He concluded with a fit of coughing which seemed to rack him.

Dora threw back her head and laughed delightfully. "Don't you apologize!" she said. "*I* didn't when I said it seemed to me that we've gone walking so often, when in reality it's only four or five times altogether. I think I can explain, though: I think it came partly from a feeling I have that I can rely on you—that you're a good, solid, reliable sort of person. I remember from the time we were little children, you always had a sort of worried, honest look in school; and you used to make a dent in your forehead—you meant it for a frown— whenever I caught your eye. You hated me so honestly, and you were so honestly afraid I wouldn't see it!"

"Oh, no—no—"

"Oh, yes—yes!" she laughed, then grew serious. "My feeling about you—that you were a person to be relied on, I mean— I think it began that evening in our freshman year, after the *Lusitania*, when I stopped you on campus and you went with me, and I couldn't help crying, and you were so nice and quiet. I hardly realized then that it was the first time we'd ever really talked together—of course *I* did all the talking!—and yet we'd known each other so many years. I thought of it afterward. But what gave me such a different view of you, I'd always thought you were one of that truculent sort of boys, always just bursting for a fight; but you showed me you'd really never had a fight in your life and hated fighting, and that you sympathized with my feeling about war." She stopped speaking to draw in her breath with a sharp sigh. "Ah, don't you remember what I've told you all along? How it keeps coming closer and closer—and now it's almost here! Isn't it *unthinkable?* And what can we do to stop it, we poor few who feel that we *must* stop it?"

"Well—" Ramsey began uncomfortably. "Of course I—I—"

"You can't do much," she said. "I know. None of us can. What can any little group do? There are so few of us among the undergraduates—and only one in the whole faculty. All the rest are for war. But we mustn't give up; we must never feel afterward that we left anything undone; we must fight to the last breath!"

"'Fight'?" he repeated wonderingly, then chuckled.

"Oh, as a figure of speech," she said, impatiently. "Our language is full of barbaric figures left over from the dark ages. But, oh, Ramsey!"—she touched his sleeve—"I've heard that Fred Mitchell is saying that he's going to Canada after Easter, to try to get into the Canadian aviation corps. If it's true, he's a dangerous firebrand, I think. Is it true?"

"I guess so. He's been talking that way some."

"But why do you *let* him talk that way?" she cried. "He's

your roommate; surely you have more influence with him than anybody else has. Couldn't you—"

He shook his head slowly, while upon his face the faintly indicated modellings of a grin hinted of an inner laughter at some surreptitious thought. "Well, you know, Fred says himself sometimes, I don't seem to be much of a talker exactly!"

"I know. But don't you see? That sort of thing is contagious. Others will think they ought to go if he does; he's popular and quite a leader. Can't you do anything with him?"

She waited for him to answer. "Can't you?" she insisted.

The grin had disappeared, and Ramsey grew red again. He seemed to wish to speak, to heave with speech that declined to be spoken and would not rouse up from his inwards. Finally he uttered words.

"I—I—well, I—"

"Oh, I know," she said. "A man—or a boy!—always hates to be intruding his own convictions upon other men, especially in a case like this, where he might be afraid of some idiot's thinking him unmanlike. But Ramsey—" Suddenly she broke off and looked at him attentively; his discomfort had become so obvious that suspicion struck her. She spoke sharply. "Ramsey *you* aren't dreaming of doing such a thing, are you?"

"What such a thing?"

"Fred hasn't influenced *you*, has he? You aren't planning to go with him, are you?"

"Where?"

"To join the Canadian aviation."

"No; I hadn't thought of doing it."

She sighed again, relieved. "I had a queer feeling about you just then—that you *were* thinking of doing some such thing. You looked so odd—and you're always so quiet, anybody might not really know what you do think. But I'm not wrong about you, am I, Ramsey?"

They had come to the foot of the steps that led up to the entrance of her dormitory, and their walk was at an end. As they stopped and faced each other, she looked at him earnestly; but he did not meet the scrutiny, his eyelids fell.

"I'm not wrong, am I, Ramsey?"

"About what?" he murmured, uncomfortably.

"You are my friend, aren't you?"

"Yes."

"Then it's all right," she said. "That relieves me and makes me happier than I was just now, for of course if you're my friend you wouldn't let me make any mistake about you. I believe you, and now, just before I go in and we won't see much of each other for a week—if you still want me to go with you again next Sunday—"

"Yes—won't you, please?"

"Yes, if you like. But I want to tell you now that I count on you in all this, even though you don't 'talk much,' as you say;

I count on you more than I do on anybody else, and I trust you when you say you're my friend, and it makes me happy. And I think perhaps you're right about Fred Mitchell. Talk isn't everything, nobody knows that better than I, who talk so much! and I think that, instead of talking to Fred, a steady, quiet influence like yours would do more good than any amount of arguing. So I trust you, you see? And I'm sorry I had that queer doubt of you." She held out her hand. "Unless I happen to see you on the campus for a minute, in the meantime, it's good-bye until a week from to-day. So—well, so, good-bye until then!"

"Wait," said Ramsey.

"What is it?"

He made a great struggle. "I'm not influencing Fred not to go," he said. "I—don't want you to trust me to do anything like that."

"What?"

"I think it's all right for him to go, if he wants to," Ramsey said, miserably.

"You do? For him to go to *fight?*"

He swallowed. "Yes."

"*Oh!*" she cried, turned even redder than he, and ran up the stone steps. But before the storm doors closed upon her she looked down to where he stood, with his eyes still lowered, a lonely-seeming figure, upon the pavement below. Her voice caught upon a sob as she spoke.

"If you feel like that, you might as well go and enlist,

yourself," she said, bitterly. "I can't—I couldn't—speak to you again after this!"

CHAPTER XIX

It was easy enough for him to evade Fred Mitchell's rallyings these days; the sprig's mood was truculent, not toward his roommate but toward Congress, which was less in fiery haste than he to be definitely at war with Germany. All through the university the change had come: athletics, in other years spotlighted at the centre of the stage, languished suddenly, threatened with abandonment; students working for senior honours forgot them; everything was forgotten except that growing thunder in the soil. Several weeks elapsed after Dora's bitter dismissal of Ramsey before she was mentioned between the comrades. Then, one evening, Fred asked, as he restlessly paced their study floor:

"Have you seen your pacifist friend lately?"

"No. Not exactly. Why?"

"Well, for my part, I think she ought to be locked up," Fred said, angrily. "Have you heard what she did this afternoon?"

"No."

"It's all over college. She got up in the class in jurisprudence and made a speech. It's a big class, you know, over two hundred, under Dean Burney. He's a great lecturer, but he's a pacifist—the only one on the faculty—and a friend of Dora's. They say he encouraged her to make this break and led the subject around so she could do it, and then called on her for an opinion, as the highest-stand student in the class. She got up and claimed there wasn't any such thing as a legitimate cause for war, either legally or morally, and said it was a sign of weakness in a nation for it to believe that it did have cause for war.

"Well, it was too much for that little, spunky Joe Stansbury, and he jumped up and argued with her. He made her admit all the Germans have done to us, the sea murders and the land murders, the blowing up of the factories, the propaganda, the strikes, trying to turn the United States into a German settlement, trying to get Japan and Mexico to make war on us, and all the rest. He even made her admit there was proof they mean to conquer us when they get through with the others, and that they've set out to rule the world for their own benefit, and make whoever else they kindly allow to live, to work for them.

"She said it might be true, but since nothing at all could be a right cause for war, than all this couldn't be a cause of war. Of course she had her regular pacifist 'logic' working; she said that since war is the worst thing there is, why, all other evils were lesser, and a lesser evil can't be a just cause for a greater. She got terribly excited, they say, but kept right on, anyway. She said war was murder and there couldn't be any other way to look at it; and she'd heard there was already talk in the university of students thinking about enlisting, and whoever did such a thing was virtually enlisting to return murder for murder. Then Joe Stansbury asked her if she meant that she'd feel toward any student that enlisted the way she would toward a murderer, and she said, yes, she'd have a horror of any student that enlisted.

"Well, that broke up the class; Joe turned from her to the platform and told old Burney that he was responsible for allowing such talk in his lecture-room, and Joe said so far as *he* was concerned, he resigned from Burney's classes right there. That started it, and practically the whole class got up and walked out with Joe. They said Burney streaked off home, and Dora was left alone in there, with her head down on her desk—and I guess she certainly deserves it. A good many have already stopped speaking to her."

Ramsey fidgeted with a pen on the table by which he sat. "Well, I don't know," he said, slowly; "I don't know if they ought to do that exactly."

"Why oughtn't they?" Fred demanded, sharply.

"Well, it looks to me as if she was only fightin' for her principles. She believes in 'em. The more it costs a person to stick to their principles, why, the more I believe the person must have something pretty fine about 'em likely."

"Yes!" said the hot-headed Fred. "That may be in ordinary times, but not when a person's principles are liable to betray their country! We won't stand that kind of principles, I tell you, and we oughtn't to. Dora Yocum's finding that out, all right. She had the biggest position of any girl in this place, or any boy either, up to the last few weeks, and there wasn't any student or hardly even a member of the faculty that had the influence or was more admired and looked up to. She had the whole show! But now, since she's just the same as called any student a murderer if he enlists to fight for his country and his flag—well, now she hasn't got anything at all, and if she keeps on she'll have even less!"

He paused in his walking to and fro and came to a halt behind his friend's chair, looking down compassionately upon the back of Ramsey's motionless head. His tone changed. "I guess it isn't just the ticket—me to be talking this way to you, is it?" he said, with a trace of huskiness.

"Oh—it's all right," Ramsey murmured, not altering his position.

"I can't help blowing up," Fred went on. "I want to say, though, I know I'm not very considerate to blow up about her to you this way. I've been playing horse with you about her ever since freshman year, but—well, you must have understood, Ram, I never meant anything that would really bother you much, and I thought—well, I *really* thought it was a good thing, you—your—well, I mean about her, you know. I'm on, all right. I know it's pretty serious with you." He paused.

Ramsey did not move, except that his right hand still fidgeted with the pen upon the table.

"Oh—well—" he said.

"It's—it's kind of tough luck!" his friend contrived to say; and he began to pace the floor again.

"Oh—well—"

"See here, ole stick-in-the-mud," Fred broke out abruptly. "After her saying what she did— Well, it's none o' my business, but—but—"

"Well, what?" Ramsey murmured. "I don't care what you say, if you want to say anything."

"Well, I *got* to say it," Fred half groaned and half blurted. "After she said *that*—and she meant it—why, if I were in your place I'd be darned if I'd be seen out walking with her again."

"I'm not going to be," Ramsey said, quietly.

"By George!" And now Fred halted in front of him, both being huskily solemn. "I think I understand a little of what that means to you, old Ramsey; I think I do. I think I know something of what it costs you to make that resolution for your country's sake." Impulsively he extended his hand. "It's a pretty big thing for you to do. Will you shake hands?"

But Ramsey shook his head. "I didn't do it. I wouldn't ever have done anything just on account of her talkin' that way. She shut the door on me—it was a good while ago."

"She did! What for?"

"Well, I'm not much of a talker, you know, Fred," said Ramsey, staring at the pen he played with. "I'm not much of anything, for that matter, prob'ly, but I—well—I—"

"You what?"

"Well, I had to tell her I didn't feel about things the way she did. She'd thought I had, all along, I guess. Anyway, it made her hate me or something, I guess; and she called it all off. I expect there wasn't much to call off, so far as she was concerned, anyhow." He laughed feebly. "She told me I better go and enlist."

"Pleasant of her!" Fred muttered. "Especially as we know what she thinks enlisting means." He raised his voice cheerfully. "Well, that's settled; and, thank God, old Mr. Bernstorff's on his way to his sweet little vine-clad cottage home! They're getting guns on the ships, and the big show's liable to commence any day. We can hold up our heads now, and we're going to see some great times, old Ramsey boy! It's hard on the home folks—Gosh! I don't like to think of that! And I guess it's going to be hard on a lot of boys that haven't understood what it's all about, and hard on some that their family affairs, and business, and so on, have got 'em tied up so it's hard to go—and of course there's plenty that just can't, and some that aren't husky enough—but the rest of us are going to have the big time in our lives. We got an awful lot to learn; it scares me to think of what I don't know about being any sort of a rear-rank private. Why, it's a regular *profession*, like practising law, or selling for a drug house on the road. Golly! Do you remember how we talked about that, 'way back in freshman year, what we were going to do when we got out of college? You were going to be practising law, for instance, and I—well, f'r instance, remember Colburn; he was going to be a doctor, and he did go to some medical school for one year. Now he's in the Red Cross, somewhere in *Persia*. Golly!"

He paused to digest this impossibility, then chattered briskly on. "Well, there's *one* good old boy was with our class for a while, back in freshman year; I bet we won't see him in any good old army! Old rough-neck Linski that you put the knob on his nose for. Tommie Hopper says he saw him last summer in Chicago soapboxin', yellin' his head off cussin' every government under the sun, but mostly ours and the Allies', you bet, and going to run the earth by revolution and representatives of unskilled labour immigrants, nobody that can read or write allowed to vote, except Linski. Tommie Hopper says he knows all about Linski; he never did a day's work in his life—too busy trying to get the workingmen stirred up against the people that exploit 'em! Tommie says he had a big crowd to hear him, though, and took up quite a little money for a 'cause' or something. Well, let him holler! I guess we can attend to him when we get back from over yonder. By George, old Ram, I'm gettin' kind of floppy in the gills!" He administered a resounding slap to his comrade's shoulder. "It certainly looks as if our big days were walking toward us!"

He was right. The portentous days came on apace, and each one brought a new and greater portent. The faces of men lost a driven look besetting them in the days of badgered waiting, and instead of that heavy apprehension one saw the look men's faces must have worn in 1776 and 1861, and the history of the old days grew clearer in the new. The President went to the Congress, and the true indictment he made there reached scoffing Potsdam with an unspoken prophecy somewhat chilling even to Potsdam, one guesses—and then through an April night went almost quietly the steady work: we were at war with Germany.

The bugles sounded across the continent; drums and fifes played up and down the city streets and in town and village squares and through the countrysides. Faintly in all ears there was multitudinous noise like distant, hoarse cheering... and a sound like that was what Dora Yocum heard, one night, as she sat lonely in her room. The bugles and fifes and drums had been heard about the streets of the college town, that day, and she thought she must die of them, they hurt her so, and now to be haunted by this imaginary cheering—

She started. Was it imaginary?

She went downstairs and stood upon the steps of the dormitory in the open air. No; the cheering was real and loud. It came from the direction of the railway station, and the night air surged and beat with it.

Below her stood the aged janitor of the building, listening. "What's the cheering for?" she asked, remembering grimly that the janitor was one of her acquaintances who had not yet stopped "speaking" to her. "What's the matter?"

"It's a good matter," the old man answered. "I guess there must be a big crowd of 'em down there. One of our students enlisted to-day, and they're givin' him a send-off. Listen to 'em, how they *do* cheer. He's the first one to go."

She went back to her room, shivering, and spent the next day in bed with an aching head. She rose in the evening, however —a handbill had been slid under her door at five o'clock, calling a "Mass Meeting" of the university at eight, and she felt it her duty to go; but when she got to the great hall she found a seat in the dimmest corner, farthest from the rostrum.

The president of the university addressed the tumultuous many hundreds before him, for tumultuous they were until he quieted them. He talked to them soberly of patriotism, and called upon them for "deliberation and a little patience." There was danger of a stampede, he said, and he and the rest of the faculty were in a measure responsible to their fathers and mothers for them.

"You must keep your heads," he said. "God knows, I do not seek to judge your duty in this gravest moment of your lives, nor assume to tell you what you must or must not do. But by hurrying into service now, without careful thought or consideration, you may impair the extent of your possible usefulness to the very cause you are so anxious to serve. Hundreds of you are taking technical courses which should be completed—at least to the end of the term in June. Instructors from the United States Army are already on the way here, and military training will be begun at once for all who are physically eligible and of acceptable age. A special course will be given in preparation for flying, and those who wish to become aviators may enroll themselves for the course at once.

"I speak to you in a crisis of the university's life, as well as that of the nation, and the warning I utter has been made necessary by what took place yesterday and to-day. Yesterday morning, a student in the junior class enlisted as a private in the United States Regular Army. Far be it from me to deplore his course in so doing; he spoke to me about it, and in such a way that I felt I had no right to dissuade him. I told him that it would be preferable for college men to wait until they could go as officers, and, aside from the fact of a greater prestige, I urged that men of education could perhaps be more useful in that capacity. He replied that if he were useful enough as a private a commission might in time come his way, and, as I say, I did not feel at liberty to attempt dissuasion. He left to join a regiment to which he had been assigned, and many of you were at the station to bid him farewell.

"But enthusiasm may be too contagious; even a great and inspiring motive may work for harm, and the university must not become a desert. In the twenty-four hours since that young man went to join the army last night, one hundred and eleven of our young men students have left our walls; eighty-four of them went off together at three o'clock to catch an east-bound train at the junction and enlist for the Navy at Newport. We are, I say, in danger of a stampede."

He spoke on, but Dora was not listening; she had become obsessed by the idea which seemed to be carrying her to the border of tragedy. When the crowd poured forth from the building she went with it mechanically, and paused in the dark outside. She spoke to a girl whom she did not know.

"I beg your pardon—"

"Yes?"

"I wanted to ask: Do you know who was the student Doctor Corvis spoke of? I mean the one that was the first to enlist, and that they were cheering last night when he went away to be a private in the United States Army. Did you happen to hear his name?"

"Yes, he was a junior."

"Who was it?"

"Ramsey Milholland."

CHAPTER XX

Fred Mitchell, crossing the campus one morning, ten days later, saw Dora standing near the entrance of her dormitory, where he would pass her unless he altered his course; and as he drew nearer her and the details of her face grew into distinctness, he was indignant with himself for feeling less and less indignation toward her in proportion to the closeness of his approach. The pity that came over him was mingled with an unruly admiration, causing him to wonder what unpatriotic stuff he could be made of. She was marked, but not whipped; she still held herself straight under all the hammering and cutting which, to his knowledge, she had been getting.

She stopped him, "for only a moment," she said, adding with a wan profoundness: "That is, if you're not one of those who feel that I shouldn't be 'spoken to'?"

"No," said Fred, stiffly. "I may share their point of view, perhaps, but I don't feel called upon to obtrude it on you in that manner."

"I see," she said, nodding. "I've wanted to speak with you about Ramsey."

"All right."

She bit her lip, then asked, abruptly: "What made him do it?"

"Enlist as a private with the regulars?"

"No. What made him enlist at all?"

"Only because he's that sort," Fred returned briskly. "He may be inexplicable to people who believe that his going out to fight for his country is the same thing as going out to commit a mur—"

She lifted her hand. "Couldn't you—"

"I beg your pardon," Fred said at once. "I'm sorry, but I don't know just how to explain him to you."

"Why?"

He laughed, apologetically. "Well, you see, as I understand it, you don't think it's possible for a person to have something within him that makes him care so much about his country that he—"

"Wait!" she cried. "Don't you think I'm willing to suffer a little rather than to see my country in the wrong? Don't you think I'm doing it?"

"Well, I don't want to be rude; but, of course, it seems to me that you're suffering because you think you know more about what's right and wrong than anybody else does."

"Oh, no. But I—"

"We wouldn't get anywhere, probably, by arguing it," Fred said. "You asked me."

"I asked you to tell my why he enlisted."

"The trouble is, I don't think I *can* tell that to anybody who needs an answer. He just went, of course. There isn't any question about it. I always thought he'd be the first to go."

"Oh, no!" she said.

"Yes, I always thought so."

"I think you were mistaken," she said, decidedly. "It was a special reason—to make him act so cruelly."

"Cruelly!" Fred cried.

"It *was!*"

"Cruel to whom?"

"Oh, to his mother—to his family. To have him go off that way, without a word—"

"Oh, no' he'd been home," Fred corrected her. "He went home the Saturday before he enlisted, and settled it with them. They're all broken up, of course; but when the saw he'd made up his mind, they quit opposing him, and I think they're proud of him about it, maybe, in spite of feeling anxious. You see, his father was an artilleryman in the war with Spain, and his grandfather was a Colonel at the end of the War of the Rebellion, though he went into it as a private, like Ramsey. He died when Ramsey was about twelve; but Ramsey remembers him; he was talking of him a little the night before he enlisted."

Dora made a gesture of despairing protest. "You don't understand!"

"What is it I don't understand?"

"Ramsey! *I* know why he went—and it's just killing me!"

Fred looked at her gravely. "I don't think you need worry about it," he said. "There's nothing about his going that you are responsible for."

She repeated her despairing gesture. "You don't understand. But it's no use. It doesn't help any to try to talk of it, though I thought maybe it would, somehow." She went a little nearer the dormitory entrance, leaving him where he was, then turned. "I suppose you won't see him?"

"I don't know. Most probably not till we meet-if we should—in France. I don't know where he's stationed; and I'm going with the aviation—if it's ever ready! And he's with the regulars; he'll probably be among the first to go over."

"I see." She turned sharply away, calling back over her shoulder in a choked voice. "Thank you. Good-bye!"

But Fred's heart had melted; gazing after her, he saw that her proud young head had lowered now, and that her shoulders were moving convulsively; he ran after her and caught her as she began slowly to ascend the dormitory steps.

"See here," he cried. "Don't—"

She lifted a wet face. "No, no! He went in bitterness because I told him to, in my own bitterness! I've killed him! Long ago, when he wasn't much more than a child, I heard he'd said that some day he'd 'show' me, and now he's done it!"

Fred whistled low and long when she had disappeared. "Girls!" he murmured to himself. "Some girls, anyhow—

they will be girls! You can't tell 'em what's what, and you can't change 'em, either!"

Then, as more urgent matters again occupied his attention, he went on at an ardent and lively gait to attend his class in map-making.

CHAPTER XXI

That thunder in the soil, at first too deep within it to be audible, had come to the surface now and gradually became heard as the thunder of a million feet upon the training grounds. The bugles rang sharper; the drums and fifes of town and village and countryside were the drums and fifes of a war that came closer and closer to every hearth between the two oceans.

All the old symbols became symbols bright and new, as if no one had ever seen them before. "America" was like a new word, and the song "America" was like a new song. All the dusty blatancies of orating candidates, seeking to rouse bored auditors with "the old flag"; all the mechanical patriotics of school and church and club; all these time-worn flaccid things leaped suddenly into living colour. The flag became brilliant and strange to see—strange with a meaning that seemed new, a meaning long known, yet never known till now.

And so hearts that thought they knew themselves came upon ambushes of emotion and hidden indwellings of spirit not guessed before. Dora Yocum, listening to the "Star Spangled Banner," sung by children of immigrants to an out-of-tune old piano in a mission clubroom, in Chicago, found herself crying with a soul-shaking heartiness in a way different from other ways that she had cried. Among the many things she thought of then was this: That the banner the children were singing about was in danger. The great country, almost a continent, had always seemed so untouchable, so safe and sure; she had never been able to conceive of a hostile power mighty enough to shake or even jar it. And since so great and fundamental a thing could not be injured, a war for its defence had appeared to be, in her eyes, not only wicked but ridiculous. At last, less and less vaguely, she had come to comprehend something of the colossal German threat, and the shadow that touched this bright banner of which the immigrants' children piped so briskly in the mission club-room.

She had begun to understand, though she could not have told just why, or how, or at what moment understanding reached her. She began to understand that her country, threatened to the life, had flung its line those thousands of miles across the sea to stand and hold Hindenburg and Ludendorff and all their Kaisers, Kings, Dukes, and Crown Princes, their Krupp and Skoda monstrous engines, and their monstrous other engines of men made into armies. Through the long haze of misted sea-miles and the smoke of land-miles she perceived that brown line of ours, and knew it stood there that Freedom, and the Nation itself, might not perish from the earth.

And so, a week later, she went home, and came nervously to Ramsey's mother and found how to direct the letter she wanted to write. He was in France.

As the old phrase went, she poured out her heart. It seems to apply to her letter.

She wrote:

Don't misunderstand me. I felt that my bitter speech to you had driven you to take the step you did. I felt that I had sent you to be killed, and that I ought to be killed for doing it, but I knew that you had other motives, too. I knew, of course, that you thought of the country more than you did of me, or of any mad thing I would say—but I thought that what I said might have been the prompting thing, the word that threw you into it so hastily and before you were ready, perhaps. I dreaded to bear that terrible responsibility. I hope you understand.

My great mistake has been—I thought I sas so "logical"—it's been in my starting everything with a thought I'd never proven; that war is the worst thing, and all other evils were lesser. I was wrong. I was wrong, because war isn't the worst evil. Slavery is the worse evil, and now I want to tell you I have come to see that you are making war on those that make slavery. Yes, you are fighting those that make both war and slavery, and you are right, and I humbly reverence and honour all of you who are in this right war. I have come home to work in the Red Cross here; I work there all day, and all day I keep saying to myself—but I really mean to *you*—it's what I pray, and oh, how I pray it: "God be with you and grant you the victory!" For you must win and you will win.

Forgive me, oh, please—and if you will, could you write to me? I know you have things to do more important than "girls"—but oh, couldn't you, please?

This letter, which she had taken care not to dampen, as she wrote, went in slow course to the "American Expeditionary Forces in France," and finally found him whom it patiently sought. He delayed not long to answer, and in time she held in a shaking hand the pencilled missive he had sent her.

You forget all that comic talk about me enlisting because of your telling me to. I'd written my father I was going at the first chance a month and a half before that day when you said it. My mind was made up at the first time there was any talk of war, and you had about as much responsibility for my going as some little sparrow or something. Of course I don't mean I didn't pay any attention to the different things you said, because I always did, and I used to worry over it because I was afraid some day it would get you in trouble, and I'm mighty glad you've cut it out. That's right; you be a regular girl now. You always were one, and I knew it all right. I'm not as scared to write to you as I was to talk to you, so I guess you know I was mighty tickled to get your letter. It sounded blue, but I was glad to get it. You *bet* I'll write to you! I don't suppose you could have any idea how glad I was to get your letter. I could sit here and write to you all day if they'd let me, but I'm a corporal now. When you answer this, I wish you'd say how the old town looks and if the grass in the front yards is as green as it usually is, and everything. And tell me some more about everything you think of when you are working down at the Red Cross like you said. I guess I've read your letter five million times, and that part ten million. I mean where you underlined that "*you*" and what you said to yourself at the Red Cross. Oh, murder, but I was glad to read that! Don't forget about writing anything else you think of like that.

Well, I was interrupted then and this is the next day. Of course, I can't tell you where we are, because that darned censor will read this letter, but I guess he will let this much by. Who do you think I ran across in a village yesterday? Two boys from the old school days, and we certainly did shake hands a few times! It was the old foolish Dutch Krusemeyer and Albert Paxton, both of them lieutenants. I heard Fred Mitchell is still training in the States and about crazy because they won't send him over yet.

If you had any idea how glad I was to get your letter, you wouldn't lose any time answering this one. Anyhow, I'm going to write to you again every few days if I get the chance, because maybe you'll answer more than one of 'em.

But see here, cut out that "sent you to be killed" stuff. You've got the wrong idea altogether. We've got the big job of our lives, we know that, but we're going to do it. There'll be mistakes and bad times, but we won't fall down. Now you'll excuse me for saying it this way, Dora, but I don't know just how to express myself except saying of course we know everybody isn't going to get back home—but listen, we didn't come over here to get killed particularly, we came over here to give these Dutchmen h—l!

Perhaps you can excuse language if I write it with a blank like that, but before we get back we're going to do what we came for. They may not all of them be as bad as some of them—it's a good thing you don't know what we do, because some of it would make you sick. As I say, there may be quite a lot of good ones among them; but we know what they've done to this country, and we know what they mean to do to ours. So we're going to attend to them. Of course that's why I'm here. It wasn't you.

Don't forget to write pretty soon, Dora. You say in your letter—I certainly was glad to get that letter—well, you say I have things to do more important than "girls." Dora, I think you probably know without my saying so that of course while I have got important things to do, just as every man over here has, and everybody at home, for that matter, well, the thing that is most important in the world to me, next to helping win this war, it's reading the next letter from you.

Don't forget how glad I'll be to get it, and don't forget you didn't have anything to do with my being over here. That was—it was something else. And you bet, whatever happens I'm glad I came! Don't ever forget *that*!

Dora knew it was "something else." Her memory went back to her first recollection of him in school: from that time on he had been just an ordinary, everyday boy, floundering somehow through his lessons in school and through his sweethearting with Milla, as the millions of other boys floundered along with their own lessons and their own Millas. She saw him swinging his books and romping homeward from the schoolhouse, or going whistling by her father's front yard, rattling a stick on the fence as he went, care-free and masterful, but shy as a deer if strangers looked at him, and always "not much of a talker."

She had always felt so superior to him, she shuddered as she thought of it. His quiet had been so much better than her talk. His intelligence was proven now, when it came to the great test, to be of a stronger sort than hers. He was wise and good and gentle—and a fighting man! "We know what they've done to this country and what they mean to do to ours. So we're going to attend to them." She read this over, and she knew that Ramsey, wise and gentle and good, would fight like an unchained devil, and that he and his comrades would indeed and indeed do what they "came for."

"It wasn't you," he said. She nodded gently, agreeing, and knew what it was that sent him. Yet Ramsey had his own secret there, and did not tell it. Sometimes there rose, faint in his memory, a whimsical picture, yet one that had always meant much to him. He would see an old man sitting with a little boy upon a rustic bench under a walnut tree to watch the "Decoration Day Parade" go by—and Ramsey would see a shoot of sunshine that had somehow got through the walnut tree and made a bedazzlement of glinting fine lines over a spot about the size of a saucer, upon the old man's thick white hair. And in Ramsey's memory, the little boy, sitting beside the veteran, would half close his eyes, drowsily, playing that this sunshine spot was a white bird's-nest, until he had a momentary dream of a glittering little bird that dwelt there and wore a blue soldier cap on its head. And Ramsey would bring out of his memory thoughts that the old man had got into the child's head that day. "We knew that armies fighting for the Freedom of Man *had* to win, in the long run.... We were on the side of God's Plan.... Long ago we began to see hints of His Plan.... Man has to win his freedom from himself—men in the light have to fight against men in the dark.... That light is the answer.... We had the light that made us never doubt."

A long while Dora sat with the letter in her hand before she answered it and took it upon her heart to wear. That was the place for it, since it was already within her heart, where he would find it when he came home again. And she beheld the revelation sent to her. This ordinary life of Ramsey's was but the outward glinting of a high and splendid spirit, as high and splendid as earth can show. And yet it was only the life of an everyday American boy. The streets of the town were full, now, of boys like Ramsey.

At first they were just boys in uniform; then one saw that they were boys no more.

They were soldiers.

ABOUT THE AUTHOR

Newton Booth Tarkington (July 29, 1869 – May 19, 1946) was an American novelist and dramatist best known for his Pulitzer Prize-winning novels The Magnificent Ambersons and Alice Adams.

Booth Tarkington was born in Indianapolis, the son of John S. Tarkington and Elizabeth Booth Tarkington. He was named after his maternal uncle Newton Booth, then the governor of California. He first attended Purdue University but graduated from Princeton University in 1893. While at Princeton he was editor of the "Nassau Literary Magazine" and formed the Triangle Club. He was also voted the most popular man in his class. When Tarkington's class graduated in 1893 he lacked sufficient credits for a degree at Princeton, where he attended classes for two years. His later achievements, however, won him an honorary A.M. in 1899 and an honorary Litt.D. in 1918.

He was one of the most popular American novelists of his time, with The Two Vanrevels and Mary's Neck appearing on the annual best-seller lists nine times.

Tarkington donated substantially to Purdue University and has been recognized for his philanthropy. Tarkington Hall, an all-men's residence hall at Purdue, is named in honor of him.

Choose from Thousands of 1stWorldLibrary Classics By

A. M. Barnard
Ada Leverson
Adolphus William Ward
Aesop
Agatha Christie
Alexander Aaronsohn
Alexander Kielland
Alexandre Dumas
Alfred Gatty
Alfred Ollivant
Alice Duer Miller
Alice Turner Curtis
Alice Dunbar
Allen Chapman
Alleyne Ireland
Ambrose Bierce
Amelia E. Barr
Amory H. Bradford
Andrew Lang
Andrew McFarland Davis
Andy Adams
Angela Brazil
Anna Alice Chapin
Anna Sewell
Annie Besant
Annie Hamilton Donnell
Annie Payson Call
Annie Roe Carr
Annonaymous
Anton Chekhov
Archibald Lee Fletcher
Arnold Bennett
Arthur C. Benson
Arthur Conan Doyle
Arthur M. Winfield
Arthur Ransome
Arthur Schnitzler
Arthur Train
Atticus
B.H. Baden-Powell
B. M. Bower
B. C. Chatterjee
Baroness Emmuska Orczy
Baroness Orczy
Basil King
Bayard Taylor
Ben Macomber
Bertha Muzzy Bower
Bjornstjerne Bjornson

Booth Tarkington
Boyd Cable
Bram Stoker
C. Collodi
C. E. Orr
C. M. Ingleby
Carolyn Wells
Catherine Parr Traill
Charles A. Eastman
Charles Amory Beach
Charles Dickens
Charles Dudley Warner
Charles Farrar Browne
Charles Ives
Charles Kingsley
Charles Klein
Charles Hanson Towne
Charles Lathrop Pack
Charles Romyn Dake
Charles Whibley
Charles Willing Beale
Charlotte M. Braeme
Charlotte M. Yonge
Charlotte Perkins Stetson
Clair W. Hayes
Clarence Day Jr.
Clarence E. Mulford
Clemence Housman
Confucius
Coningsby Dawson
Cornelis DeWitt Wilcox
Cyril Burleigh
D. H. Lawrence
Daniel Defoe
David Garnett
Dinah Craik
Don Carlos Janes
Donald Keyhoe
Dorothy Kilner
Dougan Clark
Douglas Fairbanks
E. Nesbit
E. P. Roe
E. Phillips Oppenheim
E. S. Brooks
Earl Barnes
Edgar Rice Burroughs
Edith Van Dyne
Edith Wharton

Edward Everett Hale
Edward J. O'Biren
Edward S. Ellis
Edwin L. Arnold
Eleanor Atkins
Eleanor Hallowell Abbott
Eliot Gregory
Elizabeth Gaskell
Elizabeth McCracken
Elizabeth Von Arnim
Ellem Key
Emerson Hough
Emilie F. Carlen
Emily Bronte
Emily Dickinson
Enid Bagnold
Enilor Macartney Lane
Erasmus W. Jones
Ernie Howard Pie
Ethel May Dell
Ethel Turner
Ethel Watts Mumford
Eugene Sue
Eugenie Foa
Eugene Wood
Eustace Hale Ball
Evelyn Everett-green
Everard Cotes
F. H. Cheley
F. J. Cross
F. Marion Crawford
Fannie E. Newberry
Federick Austin Ogg
Ferdinand Ossendowski
Fergus Hume
Florence A. Kilpatrick
Fremont B. Deering
Francis Bacon
Francis Darwin
Frances Hodgson Burnett
Frances Parkinson Keyes
Frank Gee Patchin
Frank Harris
Frank Jewett Mather
Frank L. Packard
Frank V. Webster
Frederic Stewart Isham
Frederick Trevor Hill
Frederick Winslow Taylor

Friedrich Kerst
Friedrich Nietzsche
Fyodor Dostoyevsky
G.A. Henty
G.K. Chesterton
Gabrielle E. Jackson
Garrett P. Serviss
Gaston Leroux
George A. Warren
George Ade
Geroge Bernard Shaw
George Cary Eggleston
George Durston
George Ebers
George Eliot
George Gissing
George MacDonald
George Meredith
George Orwell
George Sylvester Viereck
George Tucker
George W. Cable
George Wharton James
Gertrude Atherton
Gordon Casserly
Grace E. King
Grace Gallatin
Grace Greenwood
Grant Allen
Guillermo A. Sherwell
Gulielma Zollinger
Gustav Flaubert
H. A. Cody
H. B. Irving
H.C. Bailey
H. G. Wells
H. H. Munro
H. Irving Hancock
H. R. Naylor
H. Rider Haggard
H. W. C. Davis
Haldeman Julius
Hall Caine
Hamilton Wright Mabie
Hans Christian Andersen
Harold Avery
Harold McGrath
Harriet Beecher Stowe
Harry Castlemon
Harry Coghill
Harry Houidini

Hayden Carruth
Helent Hunt Jackson
Helen Nicolay
Hendrik Conscience
Hendy David Thoreau
Henri Barbusse
Henrik Ibsen
Henry Adams
Henry Ford
Henry Frost
Henry James
Henry Jones Ford
Henry Seton Merriman
Henry W Longfellow
Herbert A. Giles
Herbert Carter
Herbert N. Casson
Herman Hesse
Hildegard G. Frey
Homer
Honore De Balzac
Horace B. Day
Horace Walpole
Horatio Alger Jr.
Howard Pyle
Howard R. Garis
Hugh Lofting
Hugh Walpole
Humphry Ward
Ian Maclaren
Inez Haynes Gillmore
Irving Bacheller
Isabel Cecilia Williams
Isabel Hornibrook
Israel Abrahams
Ivan Turgenev
J.G.Austin
J. Henri Fabre
J. M. Barrie
J. M. Walsh
J. Macdonald Oxley
J. R. Miller
J. S. Fletcher
J. S. Knowles
J. Storer Clouston
J. W. Duffield
Jack London
Jacob Abbott
James Allen
James Andrews
James Baldwin

James Branch Cabell
James DeMille
James Joyce
James Lane Allen
James Lane Allen
James Oliver Curwood
James Oppenheim
James Otis
James R. Driscoll
Jane Abbott
Jane Austen
Jane L. Stewart
Janet Aldridge
Jens Peter Jacobsen
Jerome K. Jerome
Jessie Graham Flower
John Buchan
John Burroughs
John Cournos
John F. Kennedy
John Gay
John Glasworthy
John Habberton
John Joy Bell
John Kendrick Bangs
John Milton
John Philip Sousa
John Taintor Foote
Jonas Lauritz Idemil Lie
Jonathan Swift
Joseph A. Altsheler
Joseph Carey
Joseph Conrad
Joseph E. Badger Jr
Joseph Hergesheimer
Joseph Jacobs
Jules Vernes
Julian Hawthrone
Julie A Lippmann
Justin Huntly McCarthy
Kakuzo Okakura
Karle Wilson Baker
Kate Chopin
Kenneth Grahame
Kenneth McGaffey
Kate Langley Bosher
Kate Langley Bosher
Katherine Cecil Thurston
Katherine Stokes
L. A. Abbot
L. T. Meade

L. Frank Baum
Latta Griswold
Laura Dent Crane
Laura Lee Hope
Laurence Housman
Lawrence Beasley
Leo Tolstoy
Leonid Andreyev
Lewis Carroll
Lewis Sperry Chafer
Lilian Bell
Lloyd Osbourne
Louis Hughes
Louis Joseph Vance
Louis Tracy
Louisa May Alcott
Lucy Fitch Perkins
Lucy Maud Montgomery
Luther Benson
Lydia Miller Middleton
Lyndon Orr
M. Corvus
M. H. Adams
Margaret E. Sangster
Margret Howth
Margaret Vandercook
Margaret W. Hungerford
Margret Penrose
Maria Edgeworth
Maria Thompson Daviess
Mariano Azuela
Marion Polk Angellotti
Mark Overton
Mark Twain
Mary Austin
Mary Catherine Crowley
Mary Cole
Mary Hastings Bradley
Mary Roberts Rinehart
Mary Rowlandson
M. Wollstonecraft Shelley
Maud Lindsay
Max Beerbohm
Myra Kelly
Nathaniel Hawthrone
Nicolo Machiavelli
O. F. Walton
Oscar Wilde

Owen Johnson
P.G. Wodehouse
Paul and Mabel Thorne
Paul G. Tomlinson
Paul Severing
Percy Brebner
Percy Keese Fitzhugh
Peter B. Kyne
Plato
Quincy Allen
R. Derby Holmes
R. L. Stevenson
R. S. Ball
Rabindranath Tagore
Rahul Alvares
Ralph Bonehill
Ralph Henry Barbour
Ralph Victor
Ralph Waldo Emmerson
Rene Descartes
Ray Cummings
Rex Beach
Rex E. Beach
Richard Harding Davis
Richard Jefferies
Richard Le Gallienne
Robert Barr
Robert Frost
Robert Gordon Anderson
Robert L. Drake
Robert Lansing
Robert Lynd
Robert Michael Ballantyne
Robert W. Chambers
Rosa Nouchette Carey
Rudyard Kipling
Saint Augustine
Samuel B. Allison
Samuel Hopkins Adams
Sarah Bernhardt
Sarah C. Hallowell
Selma Lagerlof
Sherwood Anderson
Sigmund Freud
Standish O'Grady
Stanley Weyman
Stella Benson
Stella M. Francis

Stephen Crane
Stewart Edward White
Stijn Streuvels
Swami Abhedananda
Swami Parmananda
T. S. Ackland
T. S. Arthur
The Princess Der Ling
Thomas A. Janvier
Thomas A Kempis
Thomas Anderton
Thomas Bailey Aldrich
Thomas Bulfinch
Thomas De Quincey
Thomas Dixon
Thomas H. Huxley
Thomas Hardy
Thomas More
Thornton W. Burgess
U. S. Grant
Upton Sinclair
Valentine Williams
Various Authors
Vaughan Kester
Victor Appleton
Victor G. Durham
Victoria Cross
Virginia Woolf
Wadsworth Camp
Walter Camp
Walter Scott
Washington Irving
Wilbur Lawton
Wilkie Collins
Willa Cather
Willard F. Baker
William Dean Howells
William le Queux
W. Makepeace Thackeray
William W. Walter
William Shakespeare
Winston Churchill
Yei Theodora Ozaki
Yogi Ramacharaka
Young E. Allison
Zane Grey